MIRACLES GALORE!

MIRACLES GALORE!

The astonishing prayer experiences of

EITHNE AMOS NUNEZ

AUTUMN
HOUSE

First published in 1997

ISBN 1-873796-67-6

Classification
1. Religion
2. Prayer

Published by
Autumn House,
Alma Park, Grantham, Lincolnshire,
NG31 9SL, England

MIRACLES GALORE!

Dedication

To my Loving Father, for His
Love to me,
To Jesus, for His Sacrifice for me,
To the Holy Spirit, for guiding
me to new life.
To my loved ones, Jaime, Clive
and Elizabeth and my two
grandchildren, Kathleen and
Richard,
*. . . these testimonies of answered
prayer are dedicated.*

Acknowledgements

I thank my friend Gerald M. Freeman who, with his wife Mary Lou, has been so helpful in his practical suggestions.

I also want to acknowledge my debt of gratitude to Clive, my son, both for his technical expertise and for his encouragement.

For their prayer support and confidence, I thank Frances Free Gielow, Marie de Hoog and Mildred Bridges.

For reading my manuscript and making helpful suggestions, as well as for his enthusiasm for my project, I thank Father Columba Breen of Glenstal Abbey in Co. Limerick, Ireland.

Most of all I acknowledge the One through whom all this has been made possible and of whom this book gives testimony.

Decatur, Georgia
February, 1997

Miracles Galore!

A vivacious, redheaded Irish girl, Eithne was brought up and educated in the strict Roman Catholic tradition. By mid-teens she had rebelled to the point of becoming a crusading atheist.

But the God in whom she did not believe had a purpose for Eithne's life. A singular set of circumstances led her to belief in God and to an acceptance of the Gospel of grace.

After her conversion, Eithne's life became one of miracles galore! From Paris, to London, to her native Ireland, to Canada, the USA and Peru, Eithne's missionary outreach was entirely dependent on divine initiative.

Eithne firmly believes in prayer power. In a compelling narrative she weaves her way through miracles of healing to miraculous circumstances by which friends, relations, acquaintances and hard-bitten opponents were helped and led to new birth.

Eithne is equally at home in the high sierras of Peru, the concrete jungles of British, Canadian and American cities and in the lush green of an Ireland in the chill shadow of the IRA. Everywhere she finds bodies and minds in need of healing, souls searching for salvation — and a God who works mightily in face of the most insuperable obstacles.

THE PUBLISHERS

MIRACLES GALORE!

CONTENTS

TOP: Eithne and her husband Jaime.

ABOVE: Evangelist Ron Halvorsen — 'He looked more like a prize fighter than a preacher, which made him appear more credible than one more saintly looking.'

LEFT: Tanya Hayes as a flower girl at Eithne and Jaime's wedding. Her story is told in the chapter 'God loves little children'.

FOREWORD

By the word of their testimony

My purpose in writing this little book of testimonies will have been completely realized if only one reader catches a glimpse of the amazing love of God for His creatures which I have discovered for myself.

As a former unbeliever in the existence of God, I have accepted the invitation to 'taste and see' that the Lord is good and I am overwhelmed. He invites testing and delights in showing Himself to those who seek Him with a humble and contrite spirit. '"Test me . . .",' He invites, '"and see if I will not throw open the floodgates of heaven and pour out so much blessing that you will not have room enough for it."'[1] Jesus assured His disciples of the Father's disposition towards them by saying: 'Fear not, little flock, for it is your Father's good pleasure to give you the kingdom.'[2]

There are many who have never had an opportunity to see God's real character at work in everyday life. I trust that these pages may offer such an opportunity and that the reader may be encouraged to prove God's love for himself or herself.

'When I was in distress, I sought the Lord; at night I stretched out untiring hands and my soul refused to be comforted. . . . You kept my eyes from closing; I was too troubled to speak. I thought about the former days, the years of long ago; I remembered my songs in the night. My heart mused and my spirit enquired:

'"Will the Lord reject us for ever?

Will he never show his favour again?
Has his unfailing love vanished for ever?
Has his promise failed for all time?
Has God forgotten to be merciful?
Has he in anger withheld his compassion?"

'Then I thought, *"To this I will appeal: ... I will remember the deeds of the Lord; yes, I will remember your miracles of long ago. I will meditate on all your works and consider all your mighty deeds."*'[3]

---

[1]Malachi 3:10. [2]Luke 12:32, KJV. [3]Psalm 77:2-12, emphasis ours.

CHAPTER ONE

The call

It was a sunny day in Paris, one of those brilliantly
clear days which defied the winter chill of December. I
was stretched out on the sofa letting the light from the
tall French window bathe me as I read the last pages of
a novel. After I had let it drop to the floor my
thoughts returned immediately to the question with
which I was preoccupied. I reviewed my life and recalled how, just over a year before, I had suffered a divorce which left emotional scars. My personal prescription and therapy was to take a sabbatical year in Paris,
to learn French and to put my life back together again.
My son Clive, who was attending college, understood
my need and encouraged me in the venture.

Attending classes every evening at L'Alliance Fran-
çaise, I shared a desk with Shawki, an Egyptian gentleman, whose life had also been shattered by divorce. We
both liked the cultural aspects of the city of Paris and
spent time visiting museums and galleries. Or we
would sit in a pavement cafe over a café-crème, or walk
in the Jardin des Plantes and admire the beautiful
floral patterns of vivid colour against the deep green
shrubs and lighter green lawns. As both of us were
over forty we were not so easily infatuated, but we
became dependent on each other to fill the loneliness
of living away from family and friends.

There were also very distinct differences between us
which we had never discussed. He was a devout

Muslim while I was an atheist and fiercely independent, a stance I had developed after a strict upbringing as a Roman Catholic. My parents had hoped that I might become a nun and towards that end they chose to send me to a convent boarding school. However, the rigid and unquestioning obedience required of us as students gave me a distorted view of the God whose service I was expected to enter, and I begged my parents to let me come home. Later as I ventured out into the real world, I became more and more confirmed in my mind that God was but an imaginary Being, created from fear in the mind of primitive man, and whose existence was but a legend passed down through tradition and ritual to the present day. I could not deny that those who believed in Him received through auto-suggestion the security from fear which they craved.

There in my Paris apartment the dilemma which preoccupied me, however, was not to do with religion but with Shawki's proposal of marriage. Rather than bringing me joy, for I really liked him, it threw me into a panic. Where would we live? His home country was Egypt; mine was Canada. Whether we chose one or the other, one of us would be a foreigner. My son was all the family I had and I couldn't imagine being in another world from his. My thoughts raced around and none of the pieces of the puzzle seemed to fit together. At the root of all my fears lay the fear of another failure. I was also aware that my independent spirit would not be tolerated in the culture of the Middle East, where women are certainly not treated as being equal with men and consequently enjoy few legal rights.

As I pondered over this dilemma a voice, clear, distinct and musical, spoke these words: 'Get up and go home and set your house in order.'

It seems strange to me now that I at no time questioned whose voice it was, nor did I ask where it came from, but the effect it had on me was electrifying. I was immediately catapulted into action. As I jumped to my feet I had only one thought, one purpose, and that was to return to Canada immediately. I reached for my suitcase, searched for my passport, phoned the airline to book the earliest available flight, all the while feeling that it was my own impulse and that I was very happy with the thought of going home to Canada. When I phoned Clive to tell him of my plans to return home he was happily surprised.

Shawki's reaction was reassuring. He felt that I was doing the right thing and that my family came before anything else. I realized once again what a nice man he really was. 'Our time will come, Inshallah', he said with conviction. His faith in Allah was characteristic of his race. 'Inshallah' or 'God's will be done' was a favourite expression of his. I knew his words cloaked his feelings, but I also felt that our plans would never have materialized.

CHAPTER TWO

Appointment with God

The temperature read -20°C in Ottawa, but the wind-chill factor made it seem more like -40. I could feel every pore tightening up as a million icy needles pierced my skin through the light European clothing I wore. 'Why did I have to come so suddenly? I could have at least waited till spring,' I said to myself a dozen times. Well, I was there and it was so good to be home again, though I realized that I had no 'home' there any more. Clive booked me into a hotel as he himself boarded at the college.

The next few months passed by quickly as we found a little house near the college and I acquired a job which I liked in public relations. The weeks were punctuated by letters postmarked Paris which I read eagerly, though Paris seemed a million miles away from Ottawa, Canada. I enrolled in some professional courses at the local university and in my spare time worked on decorating the house. Feeling an indefinable restlessness I took up yoga for a while, then dropped it. Then I tried Mind Control; and after investing in two courses I dropped that, too. It was the last week in July when I received an invitation through the letter-box to a series of lectures which caught my attention immediately as the title of the first one was: 'The Middle East Crisis'. The fact that the crisis affected Egypt, Shawki's country, and Israel, a country I had visited many years before, gave me a desire to hear what the speaker would say on the subject. Age-old animosity between these two nations had existed for centuries and created a volatile situation which at any moment could spark a full-scale war.

I called my friend Joy, to invite her to accompany me to the first meeting which was to be held that very evening in a high school auditorium. I fell in with her suggestion that we should go out for a drink or some supper afterwards.

When we entered the hallway leading to the auditorium we saw a reception table on which were stacked a number of Bibles. A young lady was handing one to each person as he or she passed by, greeting everyone with a warm smile. All my atheistic vehemence against anything religious made me stop to confront her.

'What has this to do with the Middle East Conflict?' I asked, gesturing towards the Bibles.

'The speaker is going to discuss the Middle East Crisis from the perspective of Bible prophecy,' she said sweetly; and placing one in my hand said confidently: 'You do want to check it out for yourself, don't you?'

I took the Bible meekly from her and walked towards the auditorium, muttering to my friend: 'What have we let ourselves in for here?'

Joy said, 'I think it's one of those crusades, you know?'

No, I didn't know. Neither did I know that the God I had rejected and denied over the last thirty years of my life had made an appointment to meet me in this place, and that His had been the Voice which had called me home from Paris that Sunday in December.

We agreed to stay 'just for the entertainment' and took our seats right up front. The hall began to fill up, while music played softly and a pretty young lady sang a song about her love for Jesus. At the back of the rostrum a huge screen showed the title of the lecture, 'Crisis in the Middle East', with an illustration in vivid colours of a battle with tanks, rockets and fighter planes.

When the speaker came onto the platform carrying a big black Bible, he wasn't anything as I expected. He looked more like a prize fighter than a preacher. He was tall with broad shoulders and walked very purposefully to the dais. Later he told his own story, entitled, 'From gangs to God', describing his life as a gangster on the streets of Brooklyn; and he had, indeed, been a lightweight boxer. Somehow, because of his uncharacteristic appearance, I found him more credible than someone more 'saintly' looking.

On that first night of the series he tried to convince the audience that the Bible was God's love letter to people. I was not persuaded and shrugged my shoulders at every point he made. He said that God communicated with man through the Bible. Using the screen to flash texts from the Bible to support his arguments, he said, 'God commanded . . . God pleaded . . . God spoke,' etc., and at each point elicited the same, indifferent, shoulder-shrugging response from me.

But suddenly I was galvanized into a reaction when he said that God 'reasoned' with man. I wanted to stand up and shout, 'You're a liar!' There flashed before my eyes my experience when, as a child, I would ask for a reason for this or that in my catechism class and I was always made to feel guilty of great sin for even daring to ask a question. Over and over I was told never to doubt anything I learned in religion class. My parents and the nuns were of one mind. 'You must have blind obedience,' they told me — and that was the end of the discussion.

I felt that if God gave us minds to reason with, why

wouldn't He allow us to ask questions? The speaker reiterated his point, 'God reasons with man.' Before shouting out my objections to this statement, I thought I should wait until I saw what appeared on the screen. The words which I read there burned into my heart and changed my life in a flash. I knew instinctively that God must indeed exist and was speaking to me in those words. The simple text from the Old Testament invited me to a dialogue with God, in which I would find the answers to all the questions I had stored up from my childhood and which would change me from being a hardened atheist to a humble child of God.

CHAPTER THREE

Reasoning with God

'Come now, and let us reason together, saith the Lord: though your sins be as scarlet, they shall be as white as snow; though they be red like crimson, they shall be as wool.'[1]

Like a laser beam it pierced the darkness of my mind, the words entering my consciousness and touching my inmost being.

'Come now . . . and let us reason together . . . .' My thoughts tried to adjust to the light coming from the words.

Can it be that God IS and that He desires to reason with me? I tried to grasp the implications of such an idea. Fearful that the screen would change suddenly and leave me in suspense, I reread the words rapidly while seeking their import for me.

'Though your sins be as scarlet' . . . Yes, yes, I know they are, I thought, for guilt had become a near tangible burden I had carried since I had first decided to kick over the traces of my parents' beliefs and practices.

'They shall be as white as snow.' How?

'Though they be as crimson' . . . . Yes, I know they are, I acknowledged.

'They shall be as wool.' But how can red be white, and how can sins once committed be made to vanish? Despite the many questions which remained unsolved,

I fervently hoped that this seeming impossibility could be realized in my case.

I recalled my parents' disappointment in me, the black sheep of the family. Since my record was indeed heavily marked with the errors of my life, I thought, wouldn't it be wonderful to have a clean white page, without any red marks, with my name on it? How happy this would make my family, I thought! But the reality was different. Yet the words 'white as snow' conjured up an image that gave birth to hope that even I could be freed from all the guilt and remorse that seemed to burden my life and drive me to escape reality in parties and pleasure.

As I pondered the message on the screen, I came to the conclusion that God did exist after all, for such thoughts as these could never have originated in a man's mind. I realized with awe that God was speaking these words to my own wounded heart and that He was reaching down to my level in love and compassion. I suddenly wanted to ask Him a question: 'God, if You have been there all along during my life of rebellion, why didn't You swat me like a fly and destroy me when I denied You and hated Your name all these years?'

I waited, expecting an answer.

His words came directly to my heart but were as clear as if He had spoken to me audibly.

'How could I slay you?' He said gently. 'I have died for you.'

Then, as though I were present at Calvary, I saw Jesus hanging on the cross and dying for the sins which I had committed. He had volunteered to pay for them in full in love for me. As I began to understand the amazing transaction of love between the Father and the Son in 'dying for me, while I was yet a sinner', my heart melted and tears flowed silently down my cheeks; tears of sadness and of joy blended; and as they flowed I felt the tight knot around my hardened heart loosen as hope and joy filled me. I am forgiven, healed and made new in a moment, I thought. The source of all this hope and joy was God's heart of love reaching out to the burdened sinner that I was.

'He loves me?' Yes, with a better love than I had ever known. I realized suddenly that He had always loved me and had followed me through my unwavering path when I was feeling worthless, when I was in pain, lonely, and even while I was rebellious. He had patiently waited for a moment in my life when I might be willing to respond to His pleading. I understood that His love is everlasting with neither a beginning nor an ending, for God is Everlasting and He is Love.

Amazing discovery! All that I had ever done was worthy of death, but Jesus had taken my guilt away so that it need never again burden my soul. I could start over, as though I were born again. I, Eithne, a new creature. Never was there a soul who needed this exchange more than I did. Now He seemed to be waiting for my answer. He would not force Himself upon me. I had to invite Him. Appealing to my newly-awakened conscience, He seemed to be asking me,

'What do you say, Eithne? It's your decision. Will you accept Me?'

In solemn awareness that God was waiting for my response, I replied: 'Oh, yes, dear God, yes. I want You to be my God and I want to be Your child.'

I looked around me at the other people in the hall, expecting that they might have noticed my conversation with God, but no one seemed to be aware that I had been in another world or that anything strange had occurred. Even Joy, sitting beside me, did not seem to notice that I was suddenly a new creature and not the same person with whom she had walked into the hall. On the way out, I went to return the Bible to the young lady I had so shamefully abused on my arrival, and when I found her I asked her humbly if I might borrow 'this book' until the next evening when I planned to return for the meeting. She smiled prettily and gave it into my hand as a gift, but I insisted on giving a donation for it as I was not used to such gifts. She placed a transcript of the speaker's presentation in the Bible, and I slipped it into my handbag before rejoining my friend in the lobby.

My heart was light and joyful as I came out into the sunshine of that July evening in Ottawa. Joy surprised me when she asked, 'Where shall we go for a drink?' It was so out of character with the new person I had suddenly become that I was at a loss for words.

'Oh, ah, I'm feeling a little tired. I really think I should get home and go to bed early tonight,' I said rather unconvincingly. I knew I was offending her and acting strangely. But I definitely was not going for a drink — ever again, I thought. I really did want to go home and start reading the Bible, for in it I really believed that I was going to find God's answers to all my questions.

It was past midnight yet I couldn't put the book down. I seemed possessed with the thought that if my mother had known all this, how happy it would have made her, for she had always been burdened with worries for her children.

The nuns, too, who work so hard at doing penance and saying long prayers, should be told about Jesus and the reconciliation He has made for them. I recalled how people seemed to carry their religion like a burden, based on fear of eternal punishment for their sins. If they could have only known of the sin-pardoning Saviour who had taken their guilt and death upon Himself, how happy their lives might have been! How many would ever have the privilege of hearing the joyful good news which I had heard that night, which had filled my heart with gladness and liberated me from the tyranny of fear and guilt? I determined that one day, if God would enable me, I would talk to my people about Jesus.

When I looked at the clock again it was four in the morning and in just a few hours I would have to be up to go to work, but a strange new thought intruded itself on my mind and would not give me rest until I acted on it.

I threw back the covers and fell on my knees. It had been nearly thirty years since I had prayed and the old atheistic thoughts came to mock me as I knelt there beside my bed. 'Why are you on your knees? You know there is no God. You look ridiculous kneeling there like you did as a child before you became enlightened.'

I realized that I didn't know how to pray, and though the words of a child's prayer came to my memory it was meaningless. 'I shall talk to God as I would to a person,' I said to myself.

'God, if you are like this Book says, I want to be Your child, and by the power of Jesus, who died for me, I want to start my life over again with You. Thank You for loving me even when I despised You. I praise You and thank You for the happiness You have brought to me this evening. Good-night.'

With that I got back between the sheets and fell into a dreamless sleep. When I awoke, I sensed that all my old fears had gone and in their place there was a joyful anticipation of a new life in Christ.

---

[1]Isaiah 1:18, KJV.

CHAPTER FOUR

A new creature

A conversion experience is a change in the thought patterns, motives, lifestyle, habits, conversation and friends from the old life to the new. It is not something that one can keep secret, as it touches every dimension of one's experience. The first person I told about my new life in Christ was my son Clive. As I had influenced him throughout his growing years with my own atheistic views, I could not expect him to be appreciative of his mother's becoming 'religious'. He listened patiently, probably thinking that this was a new 'fad' that I was trying out like the Yoga, a few months before, and, when I had finished, he said: 'Mom, if you must get religion then it seems to be a pretty good thing for you. But please, do me a favour; don't bore me and don't bore your friends with it.'

I respected his point of view as he was only reflecting all that I had taught him from the days before my sudden conversion. I remembered that when he was just 3 or 4 he had had a truly spiritual dimension, but I had stifled it in my effort to protect him from the scars which I had received and for which I blamed my religious upbringing.

When a letter from Shawki arrived, I laid it aside for a while before reading it. I had a feeling that my 'new love' in the Lord was outshining in brilliance the old love I had for Shawki. I wondered if he would ever change from being a Muslim and become a Christian.

When I spoke to the pastor at church about Shawki, he showed me a text in the Bible which said that believers should not be 'unequally yoked together with unbelievers'. But I put the thought aside as I didn't feel quite ready to let go of my own plans for the future.

While listening to some missionaries as they told of their experiences in soul-winning in foreign lands, I thought enviously, 'I wish I could be sent on a mission. But who would choose me with my history of rebellion against God?'

I felt strangely stirred whenever I read the text in Isaiah: '"Whom shall I send? And who will go for us?" And I said: "Here I am. Send me!"'[1]

When I had been back in Canada two years, Clive moved into his own place and, while I liked my work, I began to miss Paris and Shawki. I decided that if I could sell the house which was by then looking very good after all my efforts and renovations, I would return to Paris to live. I was hoping that by a miracle the Lord would change Shawki and make us missionaries in some part of the world. Like an answer to prayer, I got three offers for the house within one week, and took this as a sign of God's approval of my plans to return to Paris.

From the moment we met at Charles de Gaulle airport, however, I felt that this was not from the Lord. Something intangible seemed to block our communication. We felt like strangers to each other. We soon found that everything we had once shared in common seemed to divide us now. I thought of our promises to each other and realized that pledges are like ropes of sand unless God gives them substance, and I felt betrayed because I wanted our relationship to be stable and solid. I realized with a growing sense of insecurity that the words written back and forth to each other were just that, words. They had no power to accomplish what they said.

I cried for broken dreams and things that might have been, and I watched Shawki's face become sombre and strained. We did all the things we used to do before I left for Canada: we had picnics in the park or on the banks of the Seine; we walked along the boulevards, stopping for a café-crème at a pavement cafe. But there was no happy chatter, only a forced gaiety with periods of silence which accentuated the more starkly how much our relationship had changed.

More than anything I felt a gaping void where I had once been filled with the joy of the Lord, and I was convinced that unless the Lord's grace and favour was with me everything else was dead. I knew without a doubt that the only way to have reconciliation with my Lord was to leave Paris and Shawki. Yet I hesitated to make that move.

Wrestling with God in prayer one morning, I confessed my sin and said, 'OK, God, I know that coming back to Paris was my idea. If this relationship is going to cost me your beautiful peace, then please help me to leave right away.'

Immediately, I felt that overwhelming peace and joy that I had lost return and bathe my spirit, and I got off my knees ready to depart as soon as I could. Once again I understood the way God was dealing with me. He did not try to force that decision, but let me see the difference between having His Spirit with me and being separated from Him. He waited for me to make up my own mind, and when I did He blessed me with that warm spirit of love and peace once again. These words seemed like His direction to me: '" . . . I am the Lord your God, who teaches you what is best for you, who directs you in the way you should go. If only you had paid attention to my commands, your peace would have been as a river." "[2]

Within a week I left Paris for the second time. This time we made no promises to each other. As the train pulled out of Gare de Lyon, I watched Shawki's form diminish as the distance separated us, and I was aware that God had intervened in my life because He loved me and He knew best. He would, eventually, heal my sadness and accomplish His purpose for my life, and with this I was content.

---

[1]Isaiah 6:8. [2]Isaiah 48:17, 18.

CHAPTER FIVE

Ireland

Driving along the narrow country roads towards the
west of Ireland, I felt I was a different person from the
one who had left there as a young teenager. In reviewing my life over those early years, I regretted that my
mother's cherished dream of making me a nun had
been shattered by my rebellious and contrary course.
She died before I came to know the Lord and I felt
comforted that God had honoured her sincere prayers
that I serve Him, though it was not in the way she
might have hoped, but as God had called me. When
Jesus cast out the demons which had tormented the
man of Gennesaret, He told him, '"Return home and
tell how much God has done for you."'[1]

In Ireland I found myself where my life had begun
and where my emotional knots had been formed, but
rather than feeling qualified for the mission of telling
my people what great things God had done for me, I
felt the need of spiritual healing myself. I needed to
rekindle the fires of my 'first love' for the Lord.

My father, then 94, had been alone by that time for
fifteen years. He had suffered from a series of strokes
but had recovered to the point of being able to care for
himself with the frequent visits and help of three of
his children. They, with their families, lived close by
and invited him over for meals, and took care of his
needs. His handicap was his inability to speak. The
rest of his fourteen children were scattered all over the

world and, like myself, only came home occasionally. Hence I felt privileged to be able to spend a little time with him when he had need of a full-time companion and helper.

My parents had been wonderfully blessed in their marriage and, though they lived on a small farm which only provided the bare necessities of life, they had been rich in the quality of life they enjoyed and were faithful to their religion throughout their lives.

One thing troubled my father in his latter years, and this was his fear of death. My sister counselled me not to read the obituary columns to him since all his peers had already died and many of their sons, likewise, were passing away. He knew his time was near, but he feared to die. In common with all mortals he could not be sure that he was good enough to enter Paradise on his record, nor was he content with the middle place of Purgatory, where he had been taught he would burn until he was pure enough to be transferred to Heaven to enjoy everlasting bliss. Not knowing God as a personal Friend left him with some doubts as to how he would be judged.

I was really reluctant to be my father's instructor in matters of faith, since his traditional beliefs were contrary to what I now understood of God from the Bible. Having the assurance of eternal life in Christ Jesus, I longed to be able to impart this comforting message to him; so I decided to pray earnestly for my father. When I went to bed at night I spent some time reviewing the day, giving thanks to God for all that He had done for me, and then I made my requests. As my mother had always done, I prayed for the members of our scattered family, bringing each one before the throne of Grace. Then I prayed particularly for my father who feared to die and for me myself who feared to show him the Way of Life. At this point it seemed as though suddenly the channel of communication between me and the Lord was cut.

In the silence of my own heart I felt the urgency to tell my father about Jesus and the Good News of salvation by grace. The words of Jesus kept reminding me of my duty to my father, '"I am the way and the truth and the life. No one comes to the Father except through me."'[2]

'But my father is a Catholic,' I argued, 'and he's an old man. Surely every living Catholic is not going to know the Gospel of Jesus Christ in order to go to heaven?'

There was no response to my reasoning. That night I went to bed disturbed as I thought of all the Muslims and Buddhists in the world and how Jesus had died for them all, and I wondered how many would ever know His name or of His vicarious sacrifice for them. The next day I was still disturbed as I reached for my Bible and it fell open at Ezekiel chapter 3: '"I have set you as a watchman on the walls of Zion. If you see the enemy coming and you don't sound the alarm, and my people are caught, then I will require their blood at your hands."'[3]

I recognized that the 'enemy' of God and man is death.[4] My father was close to the end of his life on this earth and I was reluctant to share the words of eternal life with him. But it seemed unfair that I might be held responsible before God if I neglected to share my knowledge with my father, so I went to my room to pray again.

'God,' I prayed, 'my father is Catholic and his parish priest is his spiritual guardian, not I.' Hearing no answer from God, I went about my work.

In a situation like this I realize that the Lord is very

patient, and while I was resisting the Holy Spirit's command to speak to my father of Jesus' substitutionary death for him God was preparing His last argument to convince me of my duty.

My sister came to visit and said: 'By the way, Friday is the first of the month and the priest will be distributing Holy Communion to the elderly in the parish. So make sure that Dad is shaved and dressed for the occasion. Have a white candle ready to light the moment the priest enters with the Host.'

I was relieved to hear that my father's spiritual leader would visit him, and on the morning appointed I was ready to receive him. But at the precise moment when he should have arrived I went to hang something on the clothesline at the back of the house. In a few minutes I heard a car door close and hurried in, expecting to greet the priest at the door. I was surprised to discover that in those few minutes he had already come and gone. My father indicated that he had received the Holy Communion right at the door. I then understood that this had been the regular practice of the priest and, since my father lived alone and could not speak, my family had not been aware of the matter. No words of spiritual comfort were offered; no confession was heard; and this for an old man who lived alone and could not attend church! As yet the priest was not aware that I had come home.

This careless indifference on the part of my father's priest made me aware of why God was so insistent that I should speak to my father, for He saw his need of assurance that his soul was right with Him as he approached death. He also wanted me to see that I could not rely on the priest as my father's spiritual leader. I decided I should delay no longer and brought out my Bible which I had kept out of sight in my room.

As I thought about it, I realized that the Lord in His great love for my father had given me an order to show him the Way of Life, and I had dared to argue with Him as though I could see what was best! When I saw that God had been trying to save my father and that I had been getting in His way, I prayed, 'Dear Lord, forgive me for my stubbornness and my resistance to your Holy Spirit.'

---

[1]Luke 8:39. [2]John 14:6. [3]Ezekiel 3:17, paraphrased. [4]1 Corinthians 15:26.

CHAPTER SIX

Words of life

We sat together in front of the open hearth from which a peat fire radiated a gentle heat, and as I opened the Bible I prayed silently for guidance.

'Today, Father, I'm going to read you some good news,' I began.

I have learned by experience that before we can appreciate the gift of God to us we need to know why we need salvation through Christ; so I read to him from the book of Romans: 'For all have sinned, and come short of the glory of God.'[1] The consequence of this condition is eternal damnation or death. Then I read, 'The wages of sin is death; but the gift of God is eternal life through Jesus Christ our Lord.'[2] Death is the natural result or outcome of sin, I explained, and, since all have sinned, all must die.

In the second part, God declares that the 'gift of eternal life' is available 'through Jesus Christ our Lord'. The condemned sinner can receive the gift of pardon and eternal life instead of a death sentence for his sins, and all because of God's love for His children. A verse that explains it all is this: '"For God so loved the world that he gave his one and only Son, that whoever believes in him shall not perish but have eternal life."'[3]

As I read again from the book of John: 'Yet to all who received him, to those who believed in his name, he gave the right to become children of God — chil-

dren born not of natural descent, nor of human decision . . . but born of God,'[4] I glanced at my dad to see
if there had been any impact on him after hearing
these tremendous promises, and noticed that he appeared to be listening intently. The final verse I
planned to read was in Romans: 'There is therefore
now no condemnation to them which are in Christ
Jesus, who walk not after the flesh, but after the
Spirit.'[5]

Our study had a remarkable effect on my father. In
place of his anxiety and fear I saw the joy of the Lord
giving him strength and assurance. Whenever we were
out walking, he would pause and admire a tree as
though seeing it for the first time, though every rock
and bush within a couple of miles radius was familiar
to him since his childhood. I could see the wonder of a
child in his eyes as he saw God's handiwork in nature.
He seemed to become younger and stronger than I had
ever remembered him, and his grandchildren gathered
closer and closer to this dear old man who seemed to
have developed the trust and confidence of a child
himself as he approached his final days. Of special significance was the text: ' . . . the dead in Christ shall
rise first: then we which are alive and remain shall be
caught up together with them in the clouds, to meet
the Lord in the air: and so shall we ever be with the
Lord.'[6]

As we laid our father to rest just a few months later,
I could not be mournful as I knew that he had 'gone to
sleep' in Jesus, and that we would meet again on the
resurrection morning.

My brother John lived quite close to my father's
house, and each night as I prayed for the family members I would hear his car as he started up the engine to
go to the village for a game of billiards at the pub.

In my prayers I would say, 'Lord, turn my brother John's direction around. He's worked hard all day: help him to take his rest at home with his family and bless them with Your peace and Your salvation.'

God answered that prayer when Monica, John's wife, decided to send away for some Bible studies and began to do them on her own. Very soon she was sharing her discoveries with John and they found that the person of Jesus Christ was the One they needed: '"For there is no other name under heaven given among men by which we must be saved."'[7] They asked the Lord into their lives to guide and direct them as parents of their four lovely children. They remain faithful witnesses to Jesus and reflect His love to everyone they meet.

---

[1]Romans 3:23, KJV. [2]Romans 6:23, KJV. [3]John 3:16. [4]John 1:12. [5]Romans 8:1, KJV. [6]1 Thessalonians 4:16, 17, KJV. [7]Acts 4:12.

CHAPTER SEVEN

Self-supporting missionary

Often I have noticed how God uses timing to make an impact on His children. While I was wondering how to earn a living and at the same time be a missionary to my own people in Ireland, I received a letter from a friend in Canada, enclosing a brochure which described a career as a sales representative for a beautiful set of Children's Bible Story books. It seemed just perfectly timed to answer my thoughts on this subject and to inspire me to send in my application for this work which, I believed, might reach many people in their homes and which, if blessed by the Lord, might allow me to be independent.

I little dreamed that it would lead me all over the 'Emerald Isle'; into convents, libraries and schools, as well as into the homes of the rich and the poor. In my travels I was able to be a witness of God's love for lost sinners and tell how this love had led Jesus to come to earth in order to 'seek and save that which was lost'.

I loved to visit families in their homes, to listen to their problems and to pray for the healing of their illnesses. Some were overwhelmed with poverty and despair and these, I noticed, were happy to hear of God's love and His interest in them, while others with abundance seemed to care little for the things of Heaven. The Holy Spirit seemed to guide me to the ones I should get close to, giving practical help where I could and counselling when He gave me words to share.

There was one young couple whom I shall never forget. Bill was a 24-year-old alcoholic. His wife Tina was pregnant with their third child. The day I called on them they were both sick with flu, and Bill invited me to go upstairs to talk with Tina as she was in bed. There was no carpet in any of the rooms, and when I saw this poor young woman lying on a bed without sheets or pillow cases I was shocked, and promised myself that I should return later with some of the extra items I had in my apartment.

As I became acquainted with them, I spoke of Jesus and saw how Tina's heart was touched. God desired to change their lives but He would not force Himself on them. Bill listened politely but resisted committing himself to the Lord. He seemed to be more interested in the material help I gave them than in the divine help that only Jesus could give. So I decided to visit them less frequently, while continuing to pray for them that the Lord would work on their hearts in His own way and in His own time.

A short time later Tina came to my home early one morning, very distressed. She told me that her four-month-old son Neil was in hospital with meningitis. She had just come from phoning the doctor, who told her to expect the end at any hour. She begged me to come and pray for Neil at the hospital, to which request I gladly consented. On the way there I prayed silently that God would prepare my heart and that nothing would hinder our prayer of faith. I talked to Tina about faith and told her simply, 'Faith is really believing in miracles. Since He is the Creator God, there is nothing impossible for Him.'

On arriving at the children's ward we found little Neil lying naked on a cot, just a little skeleton, crying weakly and probably weighing no more than five or six pounds. I took him in my arms, imagining how he must have missed his mummy through all the painful injections and medicines he had had to endure, and I noticed that his spine was as stiff and unyielding as a board and twisted into a Z shape. I whispered to him that his mummy loved him, that Jesus loved him and that he was going to be fine.

In the corner of the ward a nurse was feeding a baby, and I asked her if she could not try to feed this poor starving little thing. She replied that Neil couldn't swallow because of damage to his brain caused by the disease and that they had removed the intravenous feeder as it was no longer effective.

'If you'd like to try,' she said, 'there are some baby bottles right there on the tray, and if you snap the baby's lower jaw bone against the upper, you may be able to get him to swallow some milk.' Tina and I set about doing as she suggested and we managed to snap the little jaw bone in a rhythmic fashion to simulate the action of swallowing. After about ten minutes of this, we looked and saw that half of the two ounces of milk had been consumed. Encouraged, we continued to feed Neil until the bottle was almost empty. Whispering comforting words to her little infant, his mother laid him in the cot and he fell asleep. Then it was time to turn to the Lord for the help that only He could give. I reminded Tina of the faith factor, saying, 'You know, Tina, the Bible says that the prayer of faith will heal the sick. Faith is believing that God can make your baby perfectly sound in body and mind again. When you came to my house for prayer today you were already exercising faith because you remembered what I said about Jesus who has power to raise the sick and the dying, and even those who are dead. Do you believe this, Tina?'

'I do believe,' she responded firmly.

'Then let us kneel right here and just ask God to do what He said He would.' Turning to the nurse in the corner I said: 'We're going to pray for the recovery of Neil. I hope this does not disturb you.'

'Oh, no, go ahead,' she replied as she continued to feed the baby.

I spoke to God as I would to a friend and I said that He must have had a purpose for Neil's life when He brought him to birth just four months previously. As the Creator He knows every cell in our bodies and therefore could see better than any doctor exactly where little Neil's brain had been affected by the meningitis and how it could be set right. I asked Him to show the doctors that He alone had power over death, and then I ended my prayer with this plea:

'Father, Tina and I are here to plead for the life of this child and we come in the name of Jesus who told us to ask anything in His name. Show the physicians here at the hospital that You are the Great Physician, and show his parents, Bill and Tina, that you are the God of Power and Love. We ask according to Your will and in Jesus' name. Amen.'

We left little Neil still sleeping and went towards home. Tina was comforted and felt assured that God had heard our prayer. I told her to continue petitioning God in Jesus' name and that I would, too.

Because I was going overseas that very afternoon, I was not to hear the end of that story until I returned three weeks later. In my travels I never failed to pray for the pathetic little bag of bones I had seen lying in that hospital cot.

While in the USA I stayed with a doctor and his wife and, after describing Neil's condition, I asked him for his opinion. I also described the home and the family and their poverty. My medical friend shook his head and said it would be better for the child to die. Shocked to hear him say that, I argued that surely life is better than death. He said that considering the poverty in the home and the kind of brain damage that I described, it seemed to him that if the child were to live he would remain a vegetable for life and be a great additional burden on the family.

Seeing my dismay, he said that he was having a paediatrician come to visit that evening and that she would give me a second opinion. When I repeated the description of the symptoms to her, she confirmed his opinion. After retiring to my room I prayed that God, who is more powerful than human medical experts, would touch Neil and heal him.

When I returned home I went straight to the hospital to see whether the baby was still recovering, but he was no longer there.

'Have there been any deaths in the last three weeks?' I asked the receptionist a little fearfully.

'No, not in the infants' ward, anyway,' she assured me.

The child must be at home, I decided, and went there that evening.

Before I opened the gate that led to the little front path, Tina had seen me through the window and greeted me at the door as I was about to knock. She engulfed me in her arms, saying excitedly, 'Two days after you left, Neil came home. Come and see him. You won't know him,' and she led the way to the living room where the child was sleeping in a cot.

'But, Tina,' I asked a little fearfully, 'what about the brain damage?'

'What brain damage?' she replied as she threw back the covers, revealing a healthy, chubby baby who let out a strong wail on being disturbed. In his eyes of purest blue I saw the light of keen intelligence. I felt his little spine, now perfectly straight and supple, to assure myself that God had, indeed, delivered Neil perfectly sound in body and in mind.

'Have you thanked the Lord, Tina, for this wonderful miracle?' I asked her.

'I never stop praising Him, Eithne. And I would like you to come again and teach me the Bible as before. Bill told me I can study for myself.'

I left that house rejoicing in the Lord's mercy and goodness, and I remembered all the other times I had visited this couple and noticed the difference that Jesus makes in the atmosphere of a home. Sometimes God has to permit tragedy to come before He can bring peace and healing.

CHAPTER EIGHT

Jesus loves little children

One little baby I shall never forget was Tanya, Annemarie and Tom's newborn infant. It was just days after Annemarie had given birth that I visited their home and they told me that their baby was in a coma in the hospital with her lungs collapsed. The doctor had given them little hope for her life. When I told Tom and Annemarie of God's love for children and related how He had healed Neil who was dying from spinal meningitis, they were impressed but a little cynical. They glanced at each other when I offered to pray for Tanya, and I could see that there was a grain of hope, though mingled with some scepticism, especially on Tom's part.

I prayed to the Creator God, the Maker and Designer of every cell in Tanya's body, that He would step in — where doctors with their limited knowledge had failed — and heal the child. I ended my prayer with these words:

'According to Your will, Father, we ask for the life and health of little Tanya, and by doing this show her parents, Tom and Annemarie that You are God, that You really hear and answer our prayers and that nothing is too hard for You. We praise you and thank you in the worthy name of Jesus. Amen.'

I did not see them for about two weeks, then unexpectedly I met Tom in the shopping centre. He came right up to me and said, 'Your prayer was answered.

Tanya came home the following day and Annemarie has been waiting for you to visit her. She's telling everyone about the miracle of Tanya's recovery. Please go and visit her.'

This divine healing of their infant daughter led Tom and Annemarie to put their trust in the Lord. This is God's ultimate purpose when He intervenes in the lives of His children — not only to give them physical but spiritual healing. Jesus said, 'I am come that they might have life, and that they might have it more abundantly.'[1]

God worked a miracle of healing for John Paul, the 1-year-old son of a separated wife with five beautiful children. The child had chronic coeliac disease and whatever he ate caused trauma in his whole body. The doctors had tried everything they knew but now the child, reduced to a little skeleton, was not expected to live. In the midst of this crisis I visited the poverty-stricken home and the sad mother asked me to pray for her child. We prayed in faith for John Paul's life and once again God heard our prayer and the child re-covered. Certain evidence that it was God who had healed John Paul, rather than the men of medicine, was the fact that he could now eat anything without an adverse reaction.

I praise God for these evidences of His care for the poor and the sick, especially the little children, whom He loves tenderly.

---

[1]John 10:10, KJV.

CHAPTER NINE

The letter

My only son, Clive, lived many miles away from me in Canada while I was doing voluntary missionary work in Ireland. Not having heard from him in many months, I prayed for him earnestly and left the problem with the Lord. However, one November evening as I was travelling in the Dublin area, I saw dim lights reflected on the stained glass windows of the little church in Ranelagh where I came for special occasions. I was in particular need of intercessory prayer for myself and my son that evening and was glad for the small group who always met for mid-week prayer meeting in that church.

Sharing the problem with the prayer group, I confessed that I felt I had failed my son. I recalled the years in which I had raised him without the benefit of a father's help; how we had enjoyed a very close relationship. But I had been an atheist in his growing years. I had deliberately erased any sense of God from my small son's consciousness. Looking back, I realized that that had been a reaction to my own upbringing as a strict Catholic. Now, however, having had a miraculous conversion experience myself, and having turned my life over to God, I was confident that He forgave me for my past sins. Clive, however, did not have that assurance of pardon and so the consequences of my past course were still affecting his relationship with me. 'If I had to do it all over again,' I told them, 'I would live on welfare and stay home with my child rather than leave him to the care of others for the sake of a career. But it's too late now. He's 23 and doesn't communicate with me at all,' I concluded sadly, pleading for the prayers of the group for a reconciliation between myself and my son.

Each of the ladies prayed in turn and, as I heard them plead with God on my and Clive's behalf, I felt assured that God would soon work a miracle for us. Then, just as I was about to leave, one of the ladies approached me and, taking my hands in hers, she fixed a penetrating gaze upon me and said, 'Why don't you write a letter to you son and apologize?'

'Apologize?' I echoed, my tone raised slightly in alarm.

'Yes, tell him how you neglected to put him first, and how sorry you are for what you did to him, just as you told us here.' Feeling uncomfortable under that kindly gaze which seemed to search right into my guilty conscience, I turned away saying, 'He's not reading any of my letters, so it wouldn't work.'

I could not imagine confessing my weaknesses to my son, in whose eyes I had always tried to appear full of confidence and stability, even when this was just a cover-up for my fear and insecurity. Yet as I drove home that night the words 'write a letter of apology' rang insistently in my ears. They stayed with me over the next few weeks and would not leave me.

Finally, deciding that I would write a draft just to see how it would come out, but with no intention of posting it, I sat at my writing desk facing a blank page with pen poised. I prayed for divine guidance as memories long forgotten raced around my head, some of them good; others too painful to dwell upon. I acknowledged that the responsibility for leaving Clive's father was all mine. I chose to take my child and face the world alone, though I was feeling both insecure and immature myself. He had been only 2 when I had had the opportunity of emigrating to Canada. I had taken it gladly, feeling that I would make a fresh start in the 'new world'.

My pen moved a little stiffly, almost hesitantly at first, then began to race rapidly across the page keeping up with my thoughts as they tumbled out from my overflowing memory. Visions of what might have been if I had stayed, or if things had been different, floated before my mind. I felt God was reminding me that it was my duty to be frank and honest to the young man whose life I had detoured, and who might justifiably experience a crisis of identity at this vulnerable time of his life. Nevertheless, something inside me still resisted posting the letter to him. I concluded it with:

' . . . and now that I know God for myself and experience the security and peace of His presence in my life, I realize that if I had my life to do all over again, I would never have cut you off from knowing your Heavenly Father, nor would I have left your natural father, and your country of birth. And if I had to, I would live on welfare rather than leave you with strangers to care for you. I know we would have been even better off than we are now, for God would have provided for us and you would have had the security of a complete family.

'So, dearest Clive, I ask your forgiveness for the mistakes I have made in raising you. I love you and I pray that God will make things up to you for all the losses I have brought into your life. In fact, I am sure that He will make them all into blessings for you, for that is how He is.

'Your Mom, who loves you always.'

I folded the letter, placed it in an envelope, sealing and addressing it while still resisting the idea of posting it. I felt good at having written those words, and realized that there is much healing in confession and repentance.

A few days later, when posting a number of other letters and bills, I unconsciously picked up the letter from the writing desk and went to the Post Office. Just after I had dropped the assortment of envelopes in the box I realized that I had included the letter to Clive without intending to and felt apprehensive at the thought of what his reactions might be to my 'confession'. I still hoped that he would not read it. However, remembering how God would want me to do all in my power to restore our relationship, I prayed that His will, and not mine, would be done, and left the matter entirely in His hands.

A few weeks went by and, one morning, as I wondered what might have been the fate of my letter to Clive, the phone rang and I heard the international operator say, 'I have a call for you from Canada, but the line is very bad.' My heart skipped a beat as I strained to hear through the crackling of static, recognizing the dear voice of my son as he uttered incredible words, ... words of healing to a mother's heart; 'I read ... letter ... you sent ... just wanted to say ... I love you ... want to tell you ... you've always been ... a wonderful Mom to me.'

When we hung up I praised the Lord for His goodness to us. He surely knew just what Clive needed to hear, and He knew just what my letter needed to say to bring healing to our lives and erase the accumulated hurt of years that threatened to separate us.

From that point on, our relationship began to grow with love and understanding for each other and I believe that, though God has not shown me the end of the matter, I feel confident that Clive and his lovely wife Elizabeth and their two beautiful children will one day 'dwell in the house of the Lord, forever'[1] with me, as part of the redeemed family of God. This experience caused me to reflect on God's gift of repentance for the blotting out of our sins so that we may be reconciled to Him. 'If we confess our sins, he is faithful and just and will forgive us our sins and purify us from all unrighteousness.'[2]

Forgiveness comes naturally from humbling ourselves to the point of acknowledging ourselves to be at fault, and then being ready to make amends, whether it be in a changed attitude or in forgiving others as God forgives us.[3] Surely God desired our healing and so ordained mutual love and forgiveness as the perfect way to attain it.

---

[1]Psalm 23:6. [2]1 John 1:9. [3]Matthew 6:14.

CHAPTER TEN

'Whatever you have need of'

There were times during my journeys around the country as the representative for the Children's Bible Story books when I needed a miracle on my own behalf. One of those times was when my car was stolen by the IRA, a terrorist organization then very active in Ireland. I was in a Dublin city library presenting my books to the buyer, and when I returned to where I had parked the car it had gone. My loss was greater than just the car, for it contained my overnight bag, my treasured camera, my stock of books, as well as my order book and address book with special telephone numbers.

Even if I did replace the car I still could not function without the orders and notes from which I worked. I phoned Pastor John Freeman, whom I knew in the area, and when his wife answered I told her my problem and asked her to pray that I would recover everything. She invited me to their house to stay while I was in Dublin and gave me bus directions. John and Ethel Freeman were just the kind of people that God could use to comfort and support me at such a time. The pastor took me to the police station to report the loss and the officer taking my details was not too encouraging. 'Most likely they'll set fire to the car when they've finished with it or they'll use it for a bombing. You're insured, aren't you?' he asked. I nodded, but silently I was already asking God for a miracle.

At about eleven o'clock that evening we had a call from the police station, saying that they had found the car intact on a quiet street in the north of the city and that we could pick it up at any time.

The pastor drove me there immediately and, together with the police, we examined the inside and found that most of the contents were missing. I looked in the glove compartment and drew out a strange piece of cloth which we discovered to be a face mask, and I pulled out two daggers which the police wrapped in a cloth. Then we saw the IRA slogan pasted on the inside of the windscreen. On seeing this, the police decided to commandeer my car again for the night in order 'to go over it with a fine-tooth comb and get some finger prints.'

The following morning as I finally collected it from the police yard, I felt very grateful for its being intact and praised God. However, I repeated my request that He favour me by returning my other 'bits and pieces, all perhaps except the camera', I said, as I knew that my hobby of photography too often was a distraction from the real service I believed was my assignment from the Lord.

As I headed north on an appointment, I wondered how I could work without my diary and my order book, but I refused to be distressed. I knew that God could restore even these seemingly worthless things just as He had the car.

Later the same evening I received a call from Pastor Freeman in Dublin.

'You won't believe this, Eithne, but the police have delivered six plastic bags with all your things,' he said excitedly.

'What about the camera?' I asked.

'No, there's no camera I'm sorry to say.'

'That's OK, pastor. God knows what I needed most and I'm grateful that He answered our prayers. I'll pick them up tomorrow evening on my way back through Dublin.'

As I hung up I rejoiced once again that God was my personal Friend for whom nothing is too small or too large for Him to undertake on our behalf.

The next evening, as Ethel Freeman prepared us some herb tea and biscuits, the pastor recounted the story of how the police had found all those little scraps of paper. My car had indeed been used for a 'bank job' in a small town in the next county. To make room for extra passengers the bank robbers had discarded the contents of the back of the car, throwing everything over a hedge into a field of tall meadow grass. That should have been the end of them forever and might have been but for my persistent prayers that God would restore to me every scrap of paper just as He had the car.

The Lord used a lady who was out horse riding on her estate. From the height of her mount she saw a suitcase and other objects strewn about in the tall grass and suspected some sort of foul play. Immediately, she galloped her horse back to her house and called the police. They came and collected every scrap and placed them in clear plastic bags, no doubt believing they might have to mark them 'Exhibit A' in a court trial in some unknown murder case.

They pieced together the fact of the stolen car, the robbery, and the still missing items for which I was praying fervently, and delivered them to the pastor's house.

The Lord Jesus told a parable of a certain poor lady who went to a judge to receive her rights in a legal matter, but he was too busy to be bothered with her problem. She persisted in demanding to be heard until, finally, wearied of her visits, he awarded her the justice she requested. While God is not like a human judge, we should be persistent as was the widow. I believe that persistence is one of the ingredients of successful prayer. What might have been my feelings if I had been content with the return of my car only, and be satisfied with having only half of my prayer answered. Surely the Lord is happy to hear us persist for the most rather than being content with the least. One of my favourite authors wrote, 'God wants us to expect large things from Him.' Jesus made us an unlimited promise when He said: 'Ask, and it shall be given you; seek, and ye shall find; knock, and it shall be opened unto you.'[1]

---

[1] Matthew 7:7, KJV.

CHAPTER ELEVEN

A spiritual hunger

Sinead had stopped going to church during her teen years. It didn't seem to have relevance in her life. But when she got married and started to have a family she felt the need for a return to God and to religion. However, Sinead's heart was not satisfied with just the ritual of going to church and each Sunday morning she came home with the same feeling of emptiness and longing which had brought her there. Sometimes she even cried, in her loneliness, that God would come close to her; 'Show me your salvation, come close to me, I'm longing for Your love.'

Since her desire for closeness with God originates with God's Holy Spirit, He was quick to reveal Himself to Sinead. But He needs human agents as His messengers and human hands for His work. It so happened that I moved into the apartment building where Sinead lived, and she was the first person I met opening the door for me as I carried my things in from the car. A little 2-year-old followed her and from her appearance she was expecting another baby soon. We became acquainted and she told me she was moving out in a week to a larger apartment in preparation for the new baby. That might have been the end of our acquaintance had not God heard Sinead's prayer and planned that she should receive the desires of her heart. After some months had passed, I began looking for someone to do my tax returns and I was directed to Al, Sinead's husband.

I took advantage of our second meeting to get more acquainted with Sinead and told her my testimony of how I turned from atheism to God. When I saw tears roll down her cheeks, I felt sure that she was a candidate for Heaven's Grace and offered to study the Bible with her.

Sinead soaked up the Word of God and bought a Bible which she read frequently; then she told me the story of her prayer to God to show her His salvation and requested Christian baptism. She just shone with God's love and her contagious joy in the Lord has had a tremendous impact on all her family. Her mother, Ruth, and her sister Patricia and brother David, have come to the Lord, as well as her lifelong friend, Karen.

The story of how God intervened in the life of her sister is unique. A beautiful young woman in her late twenties, Patricia lived in Dublin with her husband and two children aged 2 and 4. But her husband abused Patricia, both physically and mentally, so that she lost all self esteem and, when she discovered that her husband had moved his girlfriend into their home while Patricia was visiting her parents in another town, and that the 'other woman' was her own best friend, she felt betrayed and outraged.

At the same time that Patricia was suffering this crisis her sister, Sinead, had just begun to experience the joy of the Lord in her life and phoned her frequently while praying earnestly for her and the children. But because of the distance she could not visit her. As Sinead and I met very often for Bible study, we prayed for deliverance for Patricia and her children, asking the Lord to bring her home to safety with her family. A week or so later Patricia arrived at her sister's home along with her children and told her how God had intervened in her life: 'I decided that I would commit suicide,' she said, 'but didn't know what would become of the children. While I was thinking and staring at the bookshelf I noticed in front of me the Bible which nobody in the house ever looked at and, remembering all that you had said about letting the Word of God lead me, I took it down from the shelf and just opened it at random. The words of one line popped out at me. I read, 'Ask and it shall be given you; seek, and ye shall find; knock, and it shall be opened unto you.'[1]

'I just cried out: "I'm asking you, Lord, please help me."'

'Within a few minutes it all came clear to me that I should just pack up and leave with my children, so here I am.'

If you could have seen Patricia then and were to see her now, you would not believe that she is the same person. She has demonstrated innumerable talents in arts and lettering and has exceptional skill in home decorating, cooking and gardening. Who could believe that this child of God, robbed of all self-worth, had considered killing herself! Her children are bright and talented and a credit to Patricia's life of self-sacrifice for them. God wants to lift us from the pit of despair, and it is His will that we develop the talents He has given us to His honour and glory. Patricia is enrolled at Arts School and is also teaching handicapped people in her community.

---

[1]Matthew 7:7, KJV.

CHAPTER TWELVE

Complaining to God

With missionary visits taking so much of my time, I had not sold any books during an entire week and, finding myself many miles from home and without funds, I complained to the Lord as I drove south from Belfast towards Dublin.

'Lord, this car runs on petrol and You know that costs money,' I prayed. 'I have made no sales all week and now I have no cash. I'm many miles from home and I need to restock the inventory of books since I have very few left in my car. Please tell me what to do and where to go. If I go straight on I'll reach Dublin and get some books. If I turn to the right at the next road junction, maybe I'll be able to get home late tonight. As for money, I don't know what to do. P-L-E-A-S-E, Lord, show me which road I should take!'

I slowed down for the junction. I read the names of the towns on the road signs and one of them in particular stood out more than the others; so I turned in that direction. Then I recalled that about a year previously I had visited the library in that town and talked to the assistant librarian, Andy. He had said, 'If you come next year we may be able to take some of your books, but our budget for this year has already been spent.' Somehow I had neglected to return but now I thought I might be able to reach the library before it closed.

With only ten minutes to spare I arrived at the County Library headquarters and asked the receptionist for Andy. To my great disappointment she told me that he was on holiday. She then asked if I would like to see the chief librarian.

I hesitated, feeling that I lacked the confidence to present my books to one of such authority. But she said: 'I'm sure Miss M. will be happy to see you.' With my hesitant assent she led the way and, after knocking, opened the door to a large carpeted office. The receptionist announced my name and a young woman who looked very familiar to me got up from behind her desk and came to meet me, calling me by my first name: 'Eithne, how nice to see you! I'm so glad you came to visit me.'

Then it dawned on me that it was at a booksellers' convention in another city that we had met and become acquainted. I had had a stand at the convention, displaying my books, and Marion and I had found ourselves sitting together at the end of the assembly hall, chatting. She had not revealed that she was the person responsible for about four hundred branch libraries, many of them in schools, and that she had the largest budget of any county in Ireland for the purchase of books.

Trying to excuse myself for coming late and without an appointment I said, 'Marian, I really came to see Andy, but he is on holiday.'

Smiling broadly she asked, 'Won't I do?'

'Well, I was hoping to present my books for children,' I said hesitantly.

'I'd love to see them,' she replied. 'I remember you had a nice display at the convention but at that time I was not buying.' So with a silent prayer that I make a good presentation, I showed all of the contents of my sample case and awaited the reaction of the chief librarian for the county.

'They are indeed beautiful books, just like the ones I used to read when I was a child,' she said. Then she proceeded to give me an order, larger than any I have had before or since. I was so excited I could hardly write. It seemed it would take forever to total the sale but she said, 'Send me your invoice, and you can take up to three months for delivery.'

I repacked my sample case and thanked Marion for her order and we promised to keep in touch as I left her office. In the car park, before starting up the engine, I just sat there and thanked the Lord for His goodness despite my complaining. In that amazing transaction God showed me that He is able to ' . . . supply all (my) needs according to his riches in glory by Christ Jesus.'[1]

As I headed home that evening I rejoiced in the words of Jesus which I often repeat whenever I'm tempted to be anxious about my needs: '" . . . do not worry, saying, 'What shall we eat?' or 'What shall we drink?' or 'What shall we wear?' . . . your heavenly Father knows that you need them. But seek first his kingdom and his righteousness, and all these things will be given to you as well.'"[2]

---

[1]Philippians 4:19, KJV. [2]Matthew 6:31-33.

CHAPTER THIRTEEN

Appointment with the dentist

I really wanted to go to the International Conference of Christians being held in the United States later that year. As it was a few months away, I started to pray with confidence that the Lord would provide the extra finances needed for the fare and accommodation, and I planned to pray regularly until the request was granted.

Then one morning I broke a front tooth and a visit to the dentist confirmed the worst. The cost of repairing the tooth was almost the price of a one-way ticket to America. As a result, I asked him to put a temporary crown on the tooth while I thought about it. Within a couple of weeks a second tooth broke, and again the dentist repeated the same procedure. By this time I had begun to wonder if my request to travel to the USA was really God's will for me.

In thinking over the matter, I had to ask myself why I really wanted to go. Was my request in harmony with God's will for me and would He be honoured by my going? After I was sure that there was no selfish motive for my request, I thought of Jesus' parable of the 'persistent widow' and renewed my prayers with confidence.

Suddenly things started to happen. The publishers of the Children's Bible Story books notified me that I had won a prize of a return ticket to America for having the highest sales. Then I received an invitation from a family in California, inviting me to visit them after the Conference and give a report to their church on happenings in Ireland. These two events, I concluded, were positive signs of the Lord's approval of my trip.

While I was in the USA I more fully realized how God had arranged every detail. As I enjoy telling people about God's power to overcome all difficulties when we persist in prayer, I mentioned the problem of my two front teeth, still with temporary caps, to my hostess. Early the next morning I was called to the phone, and was surprised to be speaking with the director of the Dental Hospital in town. He said, 'I believe you have some dental problems. If you can come down here and let us have a look at you we might be able to help.' I stammered something about the cost and that I couldn't afford treatment in the USA since I had no insurance coverage. He assured me there would be no charge as somebody was taking care of it.

The required treatment exceeded what I had imagined. The dentist discovered that I had a hairline crack across a number of my front teeth as a result of a car accident. If they were to be saved the teeth needed immediate expert attention. My dental treatment included five crowns and other work. God had made this dental appointment for me six months before I even knew I had a problem!

On another occasion, while I was in America at a week-long conference, I found that the cost of eating in restaurants was beyond my means; so I went on a diet of fruit and bread. On the third day I felt quite weak and hungry and, to make things worse, the most delicious smells were coming from the various cafeterias located in the halls. Before I even thought of what I was saying, I breathed out my problem to my

Father in Heaven, 'Lord, I'm hungry.'

In that instant I stepped on somebody's shoes in the crowd and, turning around to apologize, I looked into the face of my friend Mary, whom I had promised to look up while there at the conference.

She said, 'Eithne, I've been looking for you; I left messages for you at the information booth and I phoned your room but finally, just a few moments ago, I prayed, "Lord, if You want me to find her, You'll just have to help me," and here you are!'

'Was it something urgent, Mary?' I asked her, concerned.

'No, but I have a whole book of meal tickets for the cafeteria and I thought you might like to have them.'

God surely does work fast! I thought. I told Mary of my quick prayer.

'Have you had lunch yet?' I asked her.

'No,' she replied, 'let's go there right now.'

With no second invitation needed, I thanked God for His loving care for His children. He truly keeps His promise to me that, 'I shall not want'.[1]

When God speaks to us, He may use a voice, a dream, or just a strong feeling inside to indicate that He wants us to do something or go somewhere for Him.

One morning, just before I started on a trip to Northern Ireland, I had the persistent feeling that I had forgotten something. For no perceptible reason came the thought, Call your car insurance agent. Not long before, I had replaced an older model car with a new van. When I now called the agent, she said she could get me full comprehensive insurance coverage at nearly half of what I was then paying, since the category would be changed from private to commercial.

Then I left home with a thankful heart after authorizing the change.

As I was driving around a very wet and slippery corner the next day, my van went into a skid, totally out of control, and crashed into a solid stone wall. Except for a few aches in my chest and legs I had no other injuries and was able to turn off the ignition, climb out of the van and sit on the roadside waiting for help. At the hospital X-rays showed a broken sternum and superficial gashes to my legs and after four days I was released.

My new van was totally wrecked and under the new insurance coverage I was provided with a brand-new replacement without any argument. Who had impressed me to call the insurance agent before I had left the morning prior to the accident? I firmly believe God had led me to make the call.

----

[1]Psalm 23:1, KJV.

CHAPTER FOURTEEN

Miracles in a convent

While visiting many convent schools throughout the country, I became acquainted with several nuns. I attended their conferences and displayed my Children's Bible Story books. The nuns who visited my stand often invited me to call at their schools and show the books to the other teachers as well. Sometime, when they wanted the books and didn't have the money to pay, I would leave them on payment of a deposit and later they would send me a cheque. One of the sisters who had purchased the books with this arrangement wrote me a short letter, as follows:

'I enclose the final payment on the beautiful books you left with me some time ago. I didn't know how I should ever have the money, as there's always something more pressing than we have funds for. But I want to tell you what happened. I was in my room and had just prayed that God would send me the money to pay for your books, when, sitting there on the floor, I caught sight of something under my bed. It was a plastic bag with money in it — some notes and coins. Being curious, I opened it and counted the money. It contained 27.50 Irish pounds which is exactly the amount of money I owe you, plus 28 pence. The 28 pence is the price of the stamp to send it to you along with this letter. I thank God for taking care of this matter so miraculously for me. Sister J.'

On one trip I called on a large convent school and

found the principal very anxious and upset. It was not the ideal time to visit, I thought, but the Lord often makes my appointments so I greeted her cheerfully, while two little girls came to her and said, 'We looked everywhere, Sister, and we can't find them.'

'Run again and search in the halls and in the classroom. They must be found,' Sister Catherine ordered.

'Have you lost something important?' I asked the nun.

'Yes, I've lost all my keys and I'm really upset as we can't function without them.'

Then I knew that God had sent me just at this moment to talk to the sister about faith and prayer.

'Have you prayed about it, Sister?' I asked timidly.

'Of course I've prayed about it,' she answered, seeming somewhat offended that anyone should doubt her reliance on prayer. When she continued by saying that she had prayed to St Anthony, the patron saint of lost articles, I sent up a prayer so that I would know just how to share my faith with Sister Catherine in Jesus, our Powerful Intercessor.

'You know, Sister,' I said, 'I used to pray to the saints to intercede for me, but now I've found a more powerful way. I'm sure you have read in the Bible what Jesus said, "Whatsoever ye shall ask the Father in my name, he will give it you,"[1] and also "Ask, and it will be given to you; seek and you will find; knock and the door will be opened to you."[2] God promises that He will hear and answer the prayers made in the name of Jesus. If you will permit me, Sister, I'd like to pray this way for you to find your keys.'

She accepted a little reluctantly and started by making the sign of the cross over her breast. Holding her hand in mine, I bowed my head and spoke to God the Father plainly.

'Dear Father in heaven, we have been invited to ask for anything in the name of Your son, the Lord Jesus Christ. You know how important those keys are to Sister Catherine, and You know where they are, for nothing is hidden from Your eyes. We pray now that You will show the children just where those keys are and let this dear sister see that she may always rely on Your power in her prayers when they are offered through the merits of Jesus, in whose name we pray.'

Immediately, with a knock at the door, the children burst in excitedly, holding the large keyring with the keys jangling loudly, as they exclaimed, 'We've found them, Sister. We've found them!'

Still holding on to my hand tightly, Sister Catherine questioned the children about where they had found the keys and then she sent them back to their class-rooms. In wonderment she turned to me as though I were the miracle worker and said: 'Oh, you're wonderful, what a beautiful prayer . . . .'

'Sister,' I said, 'only Jesus is wonderful, and any-thing you ask of Him, believing that you will receive it, He will do it, because He has promised. I really believe that He had me come here at this moment to show you how much He wants you to rely on Him alone. In fact, Sister Catherine, the Bible says that there is only one Mediator between God and man, and that is Jesus Christ.'

Sister Catherine ordered all my books, and when-ever we met at conferences she would find me at my book stand and give me a big hug, relating all the won-derful answers she was having from her prayers to God in the name of Jesus.

Angela O'Brien spent seven years in a convent before she realized that it was not where the Lord had called her to serve. She recalls vividly the day when she made her decision to leave. She was engaged in cleaning the tall windows which overlooked the squalid housing estate in a northern industrial city in England. Always compassionate and sympathetic to the poor, Angela wished she could be down there, visiting the homes of the people and bringing comfort and encouragement to them. She would compare the relative comfort and wealth of the community of which she was a member with the poverty of the people outside the walls, and it seemed to her that there was an inconsistency between the calling to a life of self-sacrifice of the nuns and the reality of the lives of those less privileged. So rather than taking her final vows, Angela chose instead to leave the convent and take up the work of a social worker helping underprivileged children.

Eventually she met Bob O'Brien and they married and returned to their native Ireland where they raised a family of six children.

I met Angela when I was visiting her small town in County Clare. Still restlessly seeking meaning for her life but full of warmth and love, she asked me a profound question which I felt she had bottled up for many years, 'What is truth, and do you have it?' she asked. I was stunned for a moment with the seriousness of the question and recalled where the Bible tells of this same question having been asked of Jesus by Pontius Pilate. 'What is Truth?'[1]

I thought of many things I could say in response to Angela's soul hunger as she waited on my answer, but finally I said simply, 'Jesus is the Truth, Angela, and, Yes, I have that Truth.' I sent up a silent prayer that He would show me how to share the good news with this young woman whose heart was seeking the peace and security that are only to be found in Him.

In the following months we shared studies in God's Word and became close friends. Angela's knowledge and understanding of God increased with personal Bible study and prayer until one day I came by her house and found her overwhelmed with joy as, with her face beaming, she told me, 'I've found Him. I understand all now. I've made my decision to follow Jesus all the way.'

True to her missionary spirit, which is Angela's special gift from God, she never ceases to share the love of Jesus with all she meets as she tells them that only He can lift their burdens and lighten their load. One senses that Angela has, at last, found the answer to all her questions and that she experiences an inner peace and strength that can carry her through the many struggles she faces daily as she raises her children and copes with limited economic means. The Word says: '"You will seek me and find me when you seek me with all your heart."'[2]

Angela's long search is over, she has found 'Him, whom her soul loveth'.[3] His name is Jesus.

---

[1]John 16:23, KJV. [2]Matthew 7:7. [3]John 18:38. [4]Jeremiah 29:13. [5]See Song of Solomon 3:1-4, KJV.

CHAPTER FIFTEEN

His cabbage patch

My poor mother's tireless prayers for all her children, I believe, eventually led to my being brought to God's grace and favour. Of course, she had used rosary beads and invocations of saints when she prayed, but God heard her heart's anguished cry and answered her prayers as He knew best.

Now that I was privileged to know the power of prayer offered in the name of Jesus Christ whose sacrifice is like a 'sweet-smelling savour'[1] before the Father, I felt responsible to use that privilege for my family.

When my oldest brother, Joe, became the victim of a very malignant type of cancer, I redoubled my prayers for healing for him. However, I have learned from Jesus' prayer in Gethsemane to say: 'Not my will, but thine be done.'[2]

In a couple of short months Joe's life ebbed to the very brink of death. No answer seemed to come from my prayers and I was distressed. 'If He does not think it best to heal him physically, why doesn't God grant me the opportunity to speak to him of His love and of the free pardon from sin available through the sacrifice of Jesus?' I reasoned. But though Joe was sinking each day towards death, I had no sign that God was hearing my prayer. God invites us to ask Him for a sign, not a sign like the Pharisees had wanted in order that they might believe, but a sign that He was hearing and answering my prayers of faith. Then I had a strange dream.

I was in a beautiful garden where there was a cabbage patch with perfect and unblemished cabbages. Each one was giant-sized with large drops of morning dew glistening on its blue-green leaves. There were no weeds at all in the garden. Someone was with me, guiding me through the rows, and I noticed that the garden was situated just behind our old thatched house where we were born.

I asked, 'Whose is this beautiful garden?'

'It is Mine,' replied the Person beside me, and these words seemed to have great significance. When I awoke I knew that there was a message for me in this dream.

Then suddenly I understood. The garden was my family for whom I had been praying, especially Joe, now dying of cancer. The garden was the Lord's. Destressed that I could not tell my brother about the Saviour, I had forgotten that it was Jesus who died for him and that He was able to look after His own. He was able to communicate with my brother where he lay and reveal Himself directly to Joe's heart and mind.

Immediately, I wanted to go to the hospital which was located in a town about sixty miles away. Then I remembered that I had not been to the bank and it was now closed for the weekend. As I needed to fill the tank with fuel for the trip, I sent up a little request, 'Lord,' I said quietly in my heart, 'If You want me to go there today and see what You are doing for Joe, I'll need ten pounds right away.'

I put the whole thing out of my mind, and about an hour later, when I put my hand in my coat pocket, I pulled out a ten-pound note.

On arriving at the hospital I found my brother sitting up and chatting cheerfully with a nurse. When he saw me he smiled, and I sensed that he was filled with peace that the Lord gives to those whom He has chosen. Gone were the signs of death that had hovered over him for weeks. Later we prayed together and he was so happy that we could share those few words with the Lord.

Just a few days later Joe died with a peaceful smile on his face, surrounded by all his family, friends and neighbours. I look forward to meeting him again when Jesus comes.

'He will swallow up death in victory; and the Lord God will wipe away tears from off all faces . . . .'[3]

---

[1]Ephesians 5:2, KJV. [2]Luke 22:42, KJV. [3]Isaiah 25:8, KJV.

CHAPTER SIXTEEN

Troubles in Ireland

A home I visited where all the signs of poverty and neglect were evident will never be erased from my memory.

A thin, anxious little woman opened the door cautiously. She carried a baby in her arms. As she motioned for me to enter, I noticed that the house was empty of furniture except for a couple of old chairs in the kitchen where she motioned me to take one of them.

Curious to know how I might be able to help this poor woman, I asked about her family and her husband. She told me that her husband was in prison and that she had two boys at school, besides the new baby girl. She smoked constantly while she talked. I longed to touch a point where I might be able to inject some hope or joy into her life. As she sensed my sympathy she started to trust me a little, and launched into a passionate account of how her husband had been hunted and captured by the police as an IRA killer, and that it was all false. She claimed that there was no justice as he had never been charged and that he had already spent nearly a year in prison without official charges being brought against him. As she spoke I recalled the headlines which described the arrest of the infamous ringleader of the IRA who had been captured in his hideout very close to that area and I began to realize who the woman was.

She became more bitter and impassioned in her accusations of the police and in defence of her husband. She reached into her pocket and drew out a letter which looked as if it had been read over many times, and she read some parts of it to me. I was impressed with the eloquence of her husband's expressions of love for his wife as he looked forward to their reunion one day.

'These are not the words of a killer,' she said. I searched my heart for words for her, and found myself unable to break into her pleas for the innocence of her husband. The more I heard her as she accused the police of injustice, the more I became convinced that there might be some truth in her story and that her husband was an innocent man being victimized by the police, who were hungry for a 'victory' in their constant battle against the powerful IRA.

I told Mary that there was another Person who had been arrested and tried and found not guilty yet was condemned to death for crimes he did not commit. His name was Jesus and He offered Himself as a sacrifice to die for us. 'Because the grave could not hold the One who was Life itself, He rose again on the third day and now offers on our behalf the victory He gained for us through death,' I explained.

'Mary, would you like me to pray to Him, that your husband be at least granted a hearing?'

She replied that she would like that. And there, in that empty kitchen, I bowed my head and prayed earnestly that the Father in Heaven would hear and answer our prayers that this man whom his wife believed to be innocent be granted a hearing very soon. I asked this in the name of Jesus who knew what it was to suffer unjustly.

It was only two weeks later that the country was

talking once again of the ringleader, whose arrival at the court for the hearing was a major news item on television. That evening I was in another home and, as their attention was on the television, I caught a glimpse of the husband I had prayed for as he was escorted by a troop of policemen. The cameras focused for a moment on a little woman holding her baby and being held back as she struggled to get closer to her husband. It was Mary.

At the trial her husband received ten years, which many said was too light a sentence for his involvement in the IRA terrorist activities.

The next time I went to Mary's house I found it occupied by someone else, who explained that Mary had gone to live closer to her imprisoned husband. She had left a message for 'the woman who came and prayed for her'. It said would I please come and visit her whenever I could.

The address Mary had left me was in the heart of the troubled area and I really didn't think I would ever be likely to visit there for fear of the bombing or the shooting. I often thought about Mary and wondered if I would ever meet her again.

Then one day the tragic news shocked the nation. Mary, the wife of the notorious terrorist, was shot twice in the head in her home while bathing her children at bedtime. The funeral pictures were in all the papers and I gazed a long time at the saddest picture I ever saw. It showed two boys, aged about 7 and 9, gazing down on their mother's coffin as it was lowered into a grave. What can be their future? Are their hearts sown with seeds of hatred and revenge, even at such a tender age? It showed the husband, handcuffed and surrounded by police, on the edge of the crowd. What was on his mind? That he would get even with her

killers? I often think how things might have been . . . .
If Mary had put her hand in the hand of God . . . . If
I had gone to see her as she had asked me to do.

The grass has grown tall over many graves that hold
the bodies of young men and women who were caught
up in the struggles between the factions known as the
Protestants and the Catholics in Northern Ireland, but
only God knows how things might have been if those
who died 'for the cause' had known that the only True
Cause worth dying for is the Cause of Christ.

'The grave cannot praise you, death cannot sing
your praise; those who go down to the pit cannot hope
for your faithfulness.'[1]

---

[1] Isaiah 38:18.

CHAPTER SEVENTEEN

A marriage made in Heaven?

When you meet Pastor Michael Logan you are impressed with his infectious good humour and his willingness to go the extra mile to do you a service.

Mike has come a long way in his walk with the Lord. His story is another example of how Jesus follows His children — held captive and powerless to help themselves — and responds the moment they call on Him, freeing them from their bonds and restoring them to new life and freedom.

Born in Prospect, a rough neighbourhood in the city of Limerick in the mid-west of Ireland, Mike's early years were happy enough, though he sometimes chides his three older sisters for being too bossy with baby brother. He went to a Catholic school just down the road from his home and had no problem with his teachers. But, from the time of preparation for his first Confession and first Holy Communion, he began to discover the impossibility of pleasing God.

Until the tender age of 7 Mike thought of himself as holy and right with God. Then the test came. His primary class made their first confession on a Thursday and were expected to remain pure and sinless until the following Saturday. It was then that they would receive their first Communion. Mike knew that his soul had to be in the 'state of grace' . . . .

The very next morning Mike and his friend went

out to a country farm where they played on a haystack until he took a tumble and landed on the ground. Mike let out a litany of curses before he suddenly remembered his obligation to remain pure and sinless in order to receive Communion the following day. He realized with horror that he had committed a mortal sin and that if he died he would be condemned to hell fire for ever. All at once the lovely summer day turned into the darkest day of his life. Mike tried several recitations of the act of contrition by which he hoped to appease God's anger. But it felt hopeless. He was sure God would not change His mind. He stopped praying. Since he could never be as holy as God demanded, it was useless even to try, he thought. This decision altered the whole course of Mike's life.

At the age of 7 guilt weighed so heavily on Mike. He was caught up on the tragic treadmill of a sinner trying to please God by his own efforts. Soon he resented God for demanding a standard impossible to attain. For children who are naturally inclined to trust God, and whose spirit is still tender towards Him, it is tragic when this relationship is severed. It seems that nothing can heal the breach. There is a void in the child's life. Nothing can fill it. The world offers substitutes but they do not satisfy. That's just how it was with Mike Logan.

Mike tried his first alcoholic drink in an alley with friends and became an easy victim, following the example of both his father and his grandfather before him.

Mike's mother died when he was still at school. It was then that he became doubly angry with God. He had taken her to heaven leaving her children without a mother. He started missing school and generally getting into trouble. He jokes today that his main occupation during his youth was holding up the walls of the pubs of Limerick city. One night Mike was driving while drunk and crashed into the rear of a slow-moving truck. In his agony and pain he remembered words of counsel from his mother who had always been very spiritual: 'If you're ever in real need, Mike, just call on the name of Jesus.'

Mike looked down at his blood-covered body and, somehow, related this to the blood of Jesus which was shed for him. He cried out, 'Jesus, please help me, I'm so sorry.' Mike tells this story today and wonders why he said he was 'so sorry'. Was he sorry because he was near death and would meet his sins in judgement, or did he subconsciously feel remorse for his wasted life? Mike cannot tell.

What Mike was doing, in effect, was uttering the words of repentance which bring instant response from God. '"'Everyone who calls on the name of the Lord will be saved.'"'[1]

Out of the darkness of the night a pair of strong arms lifted him up, removing him from the scene of carnage and he felt safe and secure as never before.

In the hospital the first person to speak to Mike was a Christian friend who said to him, 'Mike, were you ready to die?' The words stabbed at his conscience. In the next few months he heard the question re-echo in his mind.

Mike recovered rapidly from the accident and always felt that God had intervened that night to save both his body and soul. He finally surrendered his life to Jesus and started to live, not by his own efforts to keep holy and pure, but by faith in the righteousness of Jesus on his behalf.

Evelyn lived in the same town as Mike and they met while working in the same factory.

As infants, Evelyn and her brother had been abandoned by their mother to the care of their grandparents. Evelyn suffered from acute insecurity and fear all her growing years. Soon after her grandparents died, it seemed that the children would be put in an orphanage. An aunt decided she would keep them. The aunt was married and started having her own children. Each year another baby arrived, and the threat to the two motherless children of being placed in an orphanage was renewed.

Evelyn learned to scrub floors, wash clothes and make beds. She wanted to be accepted. But the stress in her young life caused serious damage to her emotions which resulted in her becoming chronically anorexic.

Evelyn and Mike fell in love. After a short courtship they got married. Mike remarks in his humorous style, 'You might say we were the couple least likely to succeed in marriage.' They could not have children because Evelyn's condition had caused permanent physical as well as emotional damage and the doctors said she would not be likely to conceive.

One day Evelyn collapsed at work and was taken to the emergency department at the hospital in a dangerously emaciated condition. It was also at this time that Mike met with the accident. Things could not have looked worse for the young couple, yet we know that 'man's extremity is God's opportunity'.

When Mike gave his heart to Jesus after his recovery from the accident, Evelyn also hung on to the hope that God would change their lives. Together they made a new commitment to God and to each other, rededicating their lives and their marriage to God. They prayed that they might have children. God heard their prayer. In time a lovely baby daughter, whom they named Joy, was born to the couple who could never have children. Then a couple of years later little Michael joined the family. They rejoiced in all that God had done for them.

They moved from Limerick to Shannon, and found they were neighbours of another young couple who were Christians. They were invited to share Bible study with them. Mike had not yet had complete victory over the alcohol habit and, each Friday, spent his pay check at the pub in the company of his workmates.

Evelyn and the Christian couple devised ways to divert Mike from the Friday night habit by arranging for invitations for supper and other such tactics. Victory came as Mike realized that the battle was not his but the Lord's. He started participating in sports and community events. He took part in three marathons, with Evelyn and Joy and little Michael cheering from the sidelines.

Evelyn often joined Mike in his practice runs around the neighbourhood getting ready for the big city marathons. For Evelyn, life revolved around her husband and her children. She was an excellent homemaker and mother, as well as a godly influence on her husband. Hers was a faith that relied on God totally and anyone who got to know them would assume that the Logans' life was 'together', that there was nothing more they needed but to keep right on with their current pattern of life. God had prospered them. They had a lovely house and a loving family. Evelyn enjoyed her tasks around the home and Mike was happy in his work.

Yet if you asked Evelyn if she was content with her life, she would look away wistfully. Then she would say that God knew her hopes and desires. Or, perhaps, she might share with you her dream: 'I just feel that we should be serving the Lord. I would like to see Mike a pastor, and I'm preparing myself for the day when God calls him,' she would say confidently. I knew that Mike had never finished high school and that if God answered this desire of Evelyn's it would be a clear sign of His calling.

A tragic discovery was made when little Joy, then 5, was diagnosed as having a malignant tumour near her kidney. The months which followed this discovery were like a nightmare for the Logans, and caused them to ask many times, 'Why, God, why?' All their Christian friends prayed for the healing of Joy. One day when Mike and Evelyn were praying for their child, Evelyn was impressed to get olive oil and, together, they anointed Joy. Surgery was performed and a course of chemotherapy followed which caused Joy to lose her pretty golden curls and her rosy cheeks. Worse, she suffered some uncomfortable side-effects. But in all this experience the Logan family held to their faith in God, confident that He would carry them through. God rewarded their faith. Joy made a full recovery. She is now a lovely young teenager, glowing with health. The memory of her scrape with death is long forgotten. But the experience left Mike and Evelyn more determined than ever to seek God's will for their lives.

Mike began to have problems at work over trade union membership. His Christian principles forbade his participation in everything they stood for. He decided to try for admission to Bible college. It was like laying a 'fleece' before the Lord.

Mike needed to achieve university entrance requirements in his studies and asked the Lord to help him to have nothing less than outstanding results if He was calling him to be a pastor. Contrary to all expectations Mike scored 98 per cent in the Irish GED Test. Evelyn recognized God's clear leading and made plans to go to Bible college.

It was a decision which involved serious sacrifice for themselves and their children. They had to uproot from their home and attend college in England. With only enough funds to get started with Mike's education, Evelyn found work in the college kitchen to earn extra money for their sustenance. The children were enrolled in the elementary school nearby. Mike remembers a day when he cried out to the Lord to help him. He had received a note from the finance office to the effect that unless he paid his outstanding balance of nearly one thousand pounds he would not be able to register for classes the following year. Then a message arrived for him to see the academic dean right away. Usually such a summons meant bad news. Mike entered the dean's office, his head hung as if awaiting sentence. When he caught the dean's words he couldn't believe his ears. He was told that he was the recipient of a scholarship for £750.

Mike ran across the grounds to share the good news with Evelyn in the kitchen, and they praised the Lord for His goodness. The following day he received £370 from a kind member of his church who told him he had felt impressed to give this amount. The extra money left over from paying the tuition fee was just what they needed for their personal expenses for that month.

Mike and Evelyn are now ministering in the city of

Dublin, giving the message loud and clear of the real God who ' . . . so loved the world that he gave his only begotten Son, that whosoever believeth in him should not perish, but have everlasting life.'[2]

[1]Acts 2:21. [2]John 3:16, KJV.

CHAPTER EIGHTEEN

Appointment with destiny

During the ten years that had passed since my return to Ireland I received countless blessings and, especially, many answers to prayers. The Lord not only supplied my physical needs abundantly, but raised up fruits to His own glory in the two small companies of Christian believers who gathered regularly around God's Word.

I also had the satisfaction of knowing that thousands of Bible books were placed in homes, schools and libraries throughout the land. In Psalm 40 I read these words, which expressed my feelings for what God had done for me and for my countrymen in those ten years: 'Many, O Lord my God, are the wonders which Thou hast done, and Thy thoughts toward us; there is none to compare with Thee; if I would declare and speak of them, they would be too numerous to count.'[1]

Now I prayed for a change in my labours; 'Please, Lord, let me work for You in a different way for at least one year.' He arranged an invitation for me to work for six months in an evangelistic campaign in London with Evangelist Mark Finley of 'It Is Written' television fame. The next six months saw me living in a small, east-London guest house. I had to take the 'tube' every day for about an hour's journey to where we met together and prepared for our day's visiting around the city apartments and homes, as we followed up the names of those interested in attending the campaign.

I believe God is very close to the people who are lost in the life of a big city and He led us to young people who were on drugs or depressed, and to elderly people who were isolated and lonely. A vast mass of people for whom Jesus gave His life streamed into the city each morning and left it each evening. These were the ones on whom we focused our prayers and for whom we worked those six months. At the end of the evangelistic campaign six hundred people committed their lives to the Lord and became 'new creatures' in Him.

From there I went to the USA and got involved in a similar evangelistic campaign in Atlanta, Georgia, with Evangelist Ron Halvorsen, the one who had conducted the meetings when I had been converted fifteen years before in Ottawa, Canada. He had never heard my personal testimony, and now he was thrilled to see what God had been doing through me in my native land. I was happy to be a Bible worker in his campaign, inviting people to come to the meetings and studying the Scriptures with them.

One afternoon, in the balmy summer heat of Atlanta, I parked my borrowed car in the shade of a peach tree and called on a new acquaintance, Lillian. After greeting me she said, 'I was just telling my friend here about you, and here you are,' and she introduced me to a gentleman with a dark complexion who had an open Bible in his hand. He told me he was Peruvian and that he liked to share the Word of God whenever he came to visit his friend. We talked about our interest in the Bible and found that we shared the same beliefs about Jesus. He asked me if I knew anything of the Old Testament and I said that it was the foundation of the New Testament and should be understood equally. At this response he invited me to share some studies with him.

Jaime became a regular attendee at the campaign, and at the end of the series of meetings he recommitted himself to the Lord as he had already been baptized.

I noticed that from the first meeting with Jaime hardly a day passed that we did not see each other. I was sensitive to the impropriety of a woman worker always being in the company of one man, and I tried to distance myself from him, but I wasn't too successful. When his car was out of action and he phoned to have a ride to the meetings, I passed on the message to those responsible for transport, but they told me I would have to give him a ride as all the other volunteers were already overloaded. After his car was in service again, my car began to give trouble and he volunteered to be my wheels until I had it back from the garage. We had opportunities to share our experiences in the Lord, and he told me that he was praying for a committed Christian wife who loved the Lord more than she did the world.

I told him that the Lord had blessed me as a single missionary, and that I praised Him daily for the privilege of being His servant without the responsibilities of a married woman.

I showed Jaime the Bible text where Paul exhorted the new converts not to be so concerned with their marital relationships as to forget they were servants of God.

'I realize now why Paul said, "I wish that all men were as I am."[2] He was referring to his being single and free to go wherever the Lord sent him. I plan to return to Ireland just as soon as the campaign is over.'

Jaime was quiet for a moment, then he said: 'Did I tell you that I have been praying to the Lord for three things? The first is that I should find someone who could help me to study the Old Testament and I believe that the Lord sent you in answer to that prayer. The second prayer is for a truly committed wife of the Lord's choosing. I told the Lord that I had no preference as to looks, race, colour or age, but that she should love the Lord with all her heart. The third request is that He would allow me to leave this country to go on a mission.'

Now it was my turn to be quiet. I began to sense that in Jaime's mind I might be the answer to his prayer in all three aspects. I determined to discourage him from such thoughts so as not to mislead him in this sensitive area of his hopes.

'Psalm 40:5, New American Standard Bible. ²1 Corinthians 7:7.

CHAPTER NINETEEN

A fleece before
the Lord

When the campaign came to an end and I had to
return the borrowed car, Pastor Halvorsen asked Jaime
if he would volunteer to be my driver until I had concluded my visits and Bible studies in the area. A
couple who had just been baptized invited me to attend
their wedding in a town a distance of about eight
hours' drive. I asked Jaime for the loan of his car. He
agreed, but suggested that it would be better if he
could accompany me. I thanked him but said as he was
not included in the invitation I could not presume to
bring him.

The truth was, I needed some time away from him
to think things through.

I left early in the morning, and soon after
heaven opened its floodgates and I could barely see as I
drove along the highway with the car aquaplaning
dangerously.

I continued cautiously for an hour or so, then the
rear tyre went flat. It was still raining so heavily I
couldn't get out and signal for help; so I sat there with
my emergency lights flashing while it continued to
pour. Finally a car stopped and a young man changed
the wheel for the emergency spare we found in the
back. He told me I should not go far on a temporary
spare and to stop to buy a new tyre in the next town.

The rain renewed its intensity as I reached the
town, and I began to doubt that I should go any

farther. I phoned the bride's home to enquire if the weather was any better where I was going, but the answer was that the whole region seemed to be enveloped in this torrential downpour. I expressed my regrets but told them that it might be wiser for me to return to Atlanta since I was already so late and still almost a four-hour drive from them.

As I turned back towards Atlanta, the rain lessened every mile I drove in that direction, until about an hour away from Atlanta the sky was blue with no sign of a storm anywhere. When Jaime saw his car parked, he surmised that God had sent me back to him.

'I told you, Eithne,' he said when he found me later; 'God doesn't want us separated — ever again.'

The date of my departure for Ireland was close, and Jaime had begun to get through to me that God really planned that we should marry and go together on this missionary trip. I put a 'fleece' before the Lord as Gideon had done before going to fight the Midianites who were like 'swarms of locusts for number'. Gideon wanted to be sure that the Lord was sending him into battle so he asked for a sign. He would lay a fleece on the threshing-floor, and if there was dew only on the fleece and not on the ground, he would know that the Lord was indeed sending him. In the morning he found it just as he had asked: the fleece was wet and the ground dry.

Still he felt a little afraid and asked the Lord to reverse the procedure, letting the ground be wet and the fleece dry. So next morning he found the fleece was dry while the ground was wet. So with confidence he went into battle against the Midianites, with only a picked band of three hundred men, and had a spectacular victory over a vast army of the Midianites.[1]

I felt that I needed the assurance from God that He

was changing the course of my life and my service to Him by giving me a husband. I remembered when once before I had thought of marriage and God had not approved. I had to admit there were times when I wished that I had a companion in my work and service. I was happy that Jaime seemed so determined that the Lord was answering his prayers, but what I really feared was that I might be doing my will instead of God's in this matter and would reap a bitter harvest of regrets later.

I laid a 'fleece' before the Lord. I said, 'Lord, You know that I have prayed and prayed and I have not had a clear answer whether this is Your will for me. Now I ask for a sign from You. It is four o'clock in the afternoon. If this marriage is from You, make it happen that we are married by nine o'clock tomorrow morning.'

I told Jaime my request, saying, 'I believe that if God is planning that we should marry, then it should be done before we travel to Ireland.'

'The State of Georgia requires a blood test before they will issue a marriage licence,' Jaime replied.

'Well, I know the time is awfully close, but if God wants us to go ahead He will arrange it all by tomorrow morning,' I said confidently.

We went to the address of the Health Centre and found it crowded with immigrants applying for blood tests. We sat near the door for a few minutes, and then the receptionist called out for anyone who needed services other than immigration. After Jaime went to the desk and explained our quest, we were ushered past all the waiting immigrants and had our blood sample taken immediately.

'It will take just a few minutes to get your results,' the nurse said. And within fifteen minutes we had the first requirement satisfied. We found the Marriage Registry nearby, and went there with the blood results and were able to acquire the marriage licence within a few minutes. Then came the final step, the Judge's office. We were greeted by the secretary who arranged an appointment for him to marry us at 9am the following morning. All my fleeces had been answered by the Lord who was showing His approval of our plans for marriage. After the ceremony we started the drive north to prepare for our departure to Ireland. But we promised ourselves that one day we would have our vows solemnized in a truly Christian environment, maybe in Ireland.

---

[1]Judges 6:36-40.

CHAPTER TWENTY

Wedding in the park

The folk in Ireland were certainly surprised to see their wandering missionary return to them with a husband.

Jaime was well received and we enjoyed the warmth and love of the people of Ireland. Jaime became the leader of the small group of believers in our district. Day by day as the weather permitted, we ventured out together with our books. That particular winter was exceptionally cold, which we felt all the more having just come from a gentle climate. The heating system in the house was not too reliable, and I came down with a heavy cold that remained with me for weeks. During this time our income dwindled to zero. We were in need of heating fuel and prayed that God would help us to get the house warm. That evening there was a knock on the door and a coal delivery man asked where to put the bag down.

'This is the wrong house; we didn't order any fuel,' we said.

'Isn't this No. 10?' the driver asked.

'Yes, it's No. 10, but we didn't order it.'

'Well, it's paid for in advance, so it's yours.'

I had prayed to meet a certain goal in sales, but now there was no way I could ever catch up, having lost two months' work because of the flu. We prayed earnestly, and when we went out with our books we made outstanding sales. When we made up the report we were amazed to find that in just one week we had surpassed the goal we had set for three months. God is so good when we put our trust in Him.

When summer arrived we planned to have a real wedding among all our Christian believers with our dear friend, Pastor Don Vollmer, officiating, as he and Melinda were visiting Ireland from California for a couple of weeks. It was to take place in the park, where we had so often met for joint fellowship meetings between the two companies raised up from my contacts.

Before we left the house for our wedding the sky was cloudy and it was bitterly cold, while rain showers fell every few minutes. I said to Jaime, 'Let's pray that God will do a miracle with the weather for us.' We got on our knees and asked our Heavenly Father who had created the winds and the rain to banish them just for us, and we also invited Him to be present at our wedding in the park. As we drove along, I would look up at the sullen grey skies and renew my prayer for sunshine.

Just as got near to the park Jaime said, 'Look, there's a break in the clouds and there's a blue spot right above us in the sky.' I had to twist my neck to discover the tiny spot. However, it became bigger and bigger, and as we arrived in the park the sun was strong and the first thing I saw was my brother peeling off the heavy sweater he was wearing because it was too warm. Then, as though it had never rained that day, the whole sky turned a clear blue. The flower beds came alive with colour and the air resounded with the laughter of children as they climbed trees and ran about the green lawns. Jaime and I looked at each other with the same thought as we silently acknowledged that God was indeed there with us, and He had given us His sunshine as a wedding gift.

My brother John was best man and his wife Monica the matron of honour. Little Tanya, whom the Lord had healed, was dressed up as a flower girl. Sinead and her children were there and so was her sister Patricia, who had been rescued by prayer, along with her two children. Angela and her six children were there and so were Tom an Annemarie, and so many others whose lives had been touched by healing and love from the Lord.

I whispered to the pastor not to ask, 'Who will give this woman away?' as I didn't have anyone, and he agreed. But when it came to that part of the ceremony he went ahead and asked it anyway, with a mischievous twinkle in his eye, while I waited in suspense. A resounding, 'We do!' came from all the dear people who claimed me as theirs to give away in marriage.

Such is our beloved Heavenly Father. When we think we have no one in the world, He shows us a wealth of love in the people He has given us to serve. His promise is: 'Everyone who has left houses or brothers or sisters or father or mother or children or fields for my sake will receive a hundred times as much and will inherit eternal life.'[1]

For two years Jaime and I served together in Ireland. We relied on the Lord for His provision but there were times when our faith was tested. One day we had reached a crisis in faith and Jaime decided to go out and find a job as an engineer, which had been his profession. I felt that God had prior claim on his services as he had committed himself to missionary work in Ireland. While the problem remained unresolved I went to have a day of fasting and prayer at Sinead's house. We were three of us ladies and we divided our time between study of God's Word, prayer and sharing what God seemed to be telling us. At the end of the day we still had no clear answer from God.

Then Jaime arrived at the house and told us he had something to share with us. 'God spoke to me today,' he said.

He described how he was alone in the house and had started to prepare a light lunch when he heard a voice behind him, calling his name. When he turned around and saw nothing he continued to prepare his food. Then he heard these words, clear and distinct, 'Why do you rob me?'

Then he understood that he was robbing God if he refused to do that which he had dedicated himself to do, which was to serve God with his life and strength. We praised the Lord for answering our prayers by speaking directly to Jaime.

I believe there is always a response to every prayer. God has promised to answer our prayers and, though we may not see the answer in that instant, the thing is done in Heaven, and by faith we should accept that it is also done according to our prayers of faith. 'For he who promised is faithful.'[2]

---

[1]Matthew 19:29. [2]Hebrews 10:23.

CHAPTER TWENTY-ONE

Jaime's request

We decided to ask God to allow us to go to Peru for two years. Jaime had left his country to finish his degree in the States twelve years previously and, for the privilege of being allowed to go overseas for his education, his Government required that he return for a minimum of two years after graduation. Jaime, however, had other ideas and stayed on to work in the United States.

Now he began to dream of a two-year missionary stint in Peru, where he could serve the Lord and pay back his debt of two years to his Government. As for me, I was always ready for a new adventure and, never having lived in a semi-tropical climate, I felt that living in Peru would be an exciting experience. It would also give me a chance to learn Spanish and meet Jaime's people. When we made enquiries about the cost of travel to Peru, we were told that it would cost about $600 (£375) each from the US. We also enquired about a minimum budget to live on should we go and not find any means of earning a living, and we were told than an income of about $200 (£125) monthly would be sufficient for our basic necessities, provided we lived with Jaime's family and did not have to pay for accommodation.

After discussing it from every angle we decided to put it before the Lord in prayer. Jaime noted in his little pocket diary in red the date '22 February 1990', with this note: 'Asking the Lord to send us to Peru, not through our own efforts, but that we should see that it is He who sends us.'

Five months later we received an amazing answer to this prayer. We were in America to meet Jaime's parents who had come to visit his sister and her family, then we went to Georgia where my long-time friend and fellow Christian, Frances, had invited us to a retreat for the weekend. When she picked us up at the airport she was very excited and told us she had some news for us and, pulling her car to a stop at a parking area, she turned around to face us, saying: 'Eithne and Jaime, the Lord spoke to me about you. But let me begin at the beginning; I know you want to hear how it all came about. I was in my kitchen, just cleaning up, and my thoughts went to you; and as I knew you were coming from Ireland I wanted to give you some money to help with your fare, but so as to be sure, I thought I should go to my room and just talk to the Lord about it.

'I said, "Lord, I was thinking of giving $600 to help Eithne and Jaime with their fare from Ireland."

'But right there I felt a strong impression that the Lord was saying, "I didn't say $600, Frances, I said $6,000 (£3,725)."

'"Well," I said to myself, "this is all in my head, I'm just imagining it, and where would I get $6,000?"

'Then I heard a voice, this time so clear and beautiful in my ears, saying very gently, "$1,200 (£745) now and $200 a month for two years."

'I knew that I could manage this and so I got off my knees just as the phone rang. It was Teresa, the lady I had just arranged to have come and clean my house for $200 a month. She was phoning to cancel because she had too much work. Then I understood that God was telling me that the two hundred a month would be coming from doing my own housework.'

Now it was our turn to be baffled. We had forgotten our pointed prayer of five months before.

'What could this mean?' we asked ourselves. We refused to take the money until God revealed His will for it. But Frances insisted, saying, 'If you don't let me give you this cheque for twelve hundred dollars, I won't be able to do the Lord's will.' Her voice showed her concern.

Jaime assured her that it would not be cashed until we knew what God wanted us to do with it. We spent the whole day in quiet meditation and prayer, seeking the Lord's will and asking Him to show us what we should do with this money. Then Jaime took out his diary, which fell open to the page for 22 February. He read the note in red ink: 'Asking the Lord to send us to Peru, not through our own efforts, but that we should see that it is He who is sending us.' He came to show Frances and me the note and we rejoiced together to know that though we may forget, God never does.

CHAPTER TWENTY-TWO

Miracle in Lima

In going to Peru we knew we were going to experience difficulties on every side. We had heard of a cholera epidemic, of terrorism, drought, and of the masses of hungry people who settled in shanty dwellings made of cardboard, surrounding the capital, Lima. However, as bad as all this sounded, the reality that met our eyes as we travelled from the airport was an experience I shall never forget.

Horrendous odours rose from heaps of rubbish in the city streets, while homeless people scavenged among it for scraps of food. The battered 'micros' — private passenger vehicles welded together from scraps of metal — sped in and out through the traffic, honking loudly as they vied with one another to reach potential passengers at every bus stop. One could become deathly ill from drinking or eating anything from a public place. Cholera, the unseen killer, could be imbibed with a cool lemonade purchased from a vendor or even from drinking from one's tap in the kitchen. All was suspect and nothing could be touched, tasted or smelled without risk.

Knowing we were in Peru by God's will and not our own gave us confidence to live through these initial experiences. One of the texts which reminded us of His care is found in Isaiah: 'My people will live in peaceful dwelling places, in secure homes, in undisturbed places of rest.'[1]

Jaime's parents were gracious hosts and so happy to have their son home again. Their house was close to the beach at Chorillos near Lima. Abundant flowering bougainvillaea overhung the high walls which surrounded the houses, and I saw many species of flowering trees which were new to me.

The markets had abundant fruits and vegetables of every colour, size and shape, many of which I had never tasted, and so it was a time of exploration and learning for me. I noticed that in spite of the abundance of produce from the land, the constant face of poverty was everywhere. I soon began to understand that these conditions were the result of corrupt government and terrorism which drove large masses of people from their farms to settle in shanty dwellings on the edges of the capital city.

While we were wondering how we were going to survive, we received a letter from the principal of a Christian college in the neighbouring country of Colombia offering us work as computer and English teachers. We waited and prayed for work in Peru, but after a couple of weeks we began to make plans for an imminent departure for Colombia. On our last weekend we went to church where a professor from the Universidad Union Incaica, a Christian university in Nana, about twenty kilometres outside Lima, spoke about courses being offered. Later we talked and he said that he felt certain we would find work there, and invited us to visit the campus that same afternoon, which we did, accompanied by Jaime's parents.

We were all very impressed with the order and environment of the university which was such a contrast to the chaos and disarray of the streets of Lima. The campus was situated in the valley of the Rimac River, surrounded by fields luxuriant with banana trees and tall corn. The well-watered lawns and colourful flower beds gave one the impression of being in another climate. Little canals criss-crossed the grounds, and were regulated by valves to control the irrigation of the gardens. We were told some of the history of this remarkable institution which had begun as an industrial school to teach trades to worthy young Christian men and women while they learned to be missionaries. They came from all corners of Peru, highlands as well as jungle, to receive an education and learn to share the Gospel with their countrymen. Their tuition and board were paid for with their labour in the fields or in the workshops run by the institute.

Over the years modern structures replaced the older buildings, and laboratories and classrooms took the place of the workshop and fields. A vast assembly hall served for graduation ceremonies for the students of five faculties including Theology, Education, Business Administration, Nursing and Food Sciences. A new computer laboratory was about to be installed. After our delightful tour we were invited to come again to meet the Principal and the Rector.

In our meeting with them the next day, they were both very positive that if they could get the approval of the division headquarters they would be happy to hire Jaime as laboratory director and me as an English teacher. We asked how long this would take, and they said that since the headquarters was in Brazil it would take at least three weeks. We replied that we were leaving for Colombia on the following Wednesday and that we felt we should not change this plan without something more definite in view.

As we were leaving the Rector's office he offered us a ride to Lima in the university minibus, and as we had travelled there by 'micro' we gladly accepted the offer. On the way, he explained that they were having an administrative meeting and would bring up the matter of hiring us at that meeting, and they would give us their decision that very afternoon. Their decision, of course, would then have to be ratified by headquarters. Jaime and I sat outside the meeting offering up silent prayers that we might be able to stay in Lima, since Jaime's parents were elderly and were so happy to have him nearby.

Finally, the committee members emerged. The Treasurer made a thumbs up sign to us and strode over to where we were sitting and said, 'It's all arranged. You'll be staying with us.'

'But doesn't it have to be approved in Brazil?' Jaime asked.

'No, all that is finalized,' said Raul. We didn't press him for any further explanations and rejoiced that our prayers to stay in Lima had been answered miraculously.

Later, Raul told us how the matter had been finalized so quickly. On the afternoon of the meeting two of the leaders from the Brazilian headquarters were flying over Peru from Argentina. The plane they were flying in developed engine trouble and had to land in Lima. The passengers were transported to a hotel in the city and the two South American Division leaders from Brazil decided to visit the office in Miraflores, where they were invited to sit in on the meeting. Approval to hire us as regular missionary teachers was granted right there and then. We sent our apologies to Colombia. The same God who divided the Red Sea and brought water gushing from a solid rock can make miracles happen for us today. How privileged we are to be able to call this same God our Father!

---

¹Isaiah 32:18.

CHAPTER TWENTY-THREE

Prayer power

This chapter is included here in response to the many questions I receive from people who have heard me give my testimonies of answered prayer. It seems to me that many believe that God hears the prayers of some and not of others. 'God has no favourites', according to the Scriptures. 'God is no respecter of persons.'[1] He said, '"My house will be called a house of prayer for all nations."'[2]

The next few pages, I hope, will encourage those who are timid about prayer power to take heart at the experiences of others whose prayers have been answered. Prayer is a marvellous gift to us from God. It is quality time spent with our Heavenly Father, with Jesus Christ and with the Holy Spirit. It is an important time out from this world while we pause to get a glimpse of God's throne room where our prayers are kept before Him. The words of the Apostle James reveal that our prayers do count, 'The effectual fervent prayer of a righteous man availeth much.'[3]

God's prescription for successful communication with Him is found in the Bible, and this is where we shall now find answers to all our questions.

WHO INVENTED PRAYER? The origin of prayer is with God Himself. He initiated this intimate communication between the creature and the Creator as we read in the Old Testament: '"If my people, who are called by my name, will humble themselves and pray and seek my face . . . then will I hear from heaven and will forgive their sin and will heal their land." "[4]

WHAT IS PRAYER? Prayer is communicating with God heart to heart and mind to mind. It is reasoning with Him on things we don't understand: '"Come now, let us reason together," says the Lord.'[5]

Prayer is allowing our thoughts and petitions to flow from us to the very heart of God, the Creator of Heaven and earth. If such a thought is too daunting for you, you are not alone. King David also found it so and exclaimed: 'Before a word is on my tongue you know it completely, O Lord. . . . Such knowledge is too wonderful for me, too lofty for me to attain.[6]

God knows that our human nature limits our ability to reason and communicate with Him, but He reaches down to our level in order to lift us up to His.

WHAT SHOULD WE PRAY FOR? We have the example of young King Solomon who felt unable in his own power to rule over the greatest nation on earth, but he knew what he needed and to whom he could pray. He petitioned God for wisdom and God was so pleased with his choice that He sent him this reply: 'Because you have not asked for riches and honour for yourself, but have asked for wisdom to rule my people, I will also give you riches and honour and glory.'[7]

Jesus said, 'I will do whatever you ask in my name.'[8] We are also told that our 'Heavenly Father knows what we have need of.'[9]

We must remember that God does not sit on His throne just waiting to take our orders for this and for that. He would be more pleased if we could recognize what our true needs are and ask Him to grant us those things that are needful.

WHAT SHOULD BE OUR ATTITIDE IN PRAYER? When we recognize our true condition as sinners, and accept Christ's death on our behalf, we shall always come to God as humble, redeemed sinners, relying solely on the merit of Jesus' blood: 'For all have sinned and fall short of the glory of God,' and 'the wages of sin is death.'[10]

But God the Father loved us too much to leave us under sentence of eternal death: 'For God so loved the world, that he gave his only begotten Son, that whosoever believeth in him should not perish, but have eternal life.'[11]

These two verses of Scripture should keep us in an attitude of gratitude and humility before God as we approach prayer. Another indispensable attitude in prayer is faith, for: 'Without faith it is impossible to please God, because anyone who comes to him must believe that he exists and that he rewards those who earnestly seek him.'[12]

Faith is our assurance in advance of God's favour towards us and of His willingness to grant our request. When we know that we are God's own children and that it is His good pleasure to have us come near and commune with Him we may have the confidence of a child with his father, only more so, considering our Heavenly Father is also our Creator, our Redeemer, and our Lord.

WHAT IS GOD'S ATTITUDE TOWARDS US? God sympathizes with His people. The Bible says: 'He knows how we are formed, he remembers that we are dust.'[13]

Even as God was sending His chosen people into

exile for their own good, He exclaimed through Jeremiah, the prophet: '"For I know the plans I have for you . . . plans to prosper you and not to harm you, plans to give you hope and a future. Then you will call upon me and come and pray to me, and I will listen to you."'[14]

When King Hezekiah was told by the prophet that he was going to die, he turned his face to the wall and cried to the Lord. The Lord immediately sent the prophet back to the king with His message: '"'I have heard your prayer and seen your tears; I will heal you.'"'[15]

God's love is eternal and unconditional: '"I have loved you with an everlasting love; I have drawn you with loving-kindness."'[16]

WE HAVE OUR OWN ADVOCATE. We have Jesus as our advocate before the court of heaven, pleading our case: '"Until now you have not asked for anything in my name. Ask and you will receive, and your joy will be complete."'[17] '"I am the way and the truth and the life. No one comes to the Father except through me."'[18] '"And I will do whatever you ask in my name, so that the Son may bring glory to the Father. You may ask me for anything in my name, and I will do it."'[19]

The Bible assures us that in Christ we have access by faith to God: 'Since we have been justified through faith, we have peace with God through our Lord Jesus Christ, through whom we have gained access by faith into this grace.'[20] 'Let us then approach the throne of grace with confidence, so that we may receive mercy and find grace to help us in our time of need.'[21]

BECAUSE HE PROMISED. We may avail ourselves of all the beautiful promises of God to be found in His Word and claim their power for our lives. Our prayers,

then, will have power with God: '"So is my word that
goes out from my mouth: It will not return to me
empty, but will accomplish what I desire, and achieve
the purpose for which I sent it."'[22]

HOW SOON WILL THE ANSWER COME? God's
answers to prayer are always ON TIME. They will
neither be too soon nor too late. The Scriptures give
incidences of God's answers coming even while the
word was in the mouth of the petitioner.

Daniel reported: 'While I was speaking and praying,
confessing my sin and the sin of my people Israel . . .
Gabriel . . . came to me in swift flight.'[23]

In the case of King Hezekiah, we read: 'Before
Isaiah had left the middle court, the word of the Lord
came to him: "Go back and tell Hezekiah. . . . 'I have
heard your prayer.'"'[24]

I believe that God answers all prayers just as
speedily as He did Daniel's and Hezekiah's, though we
may only be aware of the results later.

PRAISE AND THANKSGIVING. Whether we can
see God's answers to our prayers or not, we should
always have an attitude of praise and thanksgiving
towards God. If we can't think of anything to be grateful for immediately, we should remember the sins of
the past and the cost of our redemption. For: '"Their
sins and lawless acts I will remember no more."'[25] '"I
have swept away your offences like a cloud, your sins
like the morning mist. Return to me, for I have
redeemed you."'[26]

If we were never to see any other blessing from
God but this, we should thank Him for His willingness to forgive and to forget our past sins and for His
gift of eternal life through Jesus, who '"loved me and
gave himself for me."'[27]

WHAT ABOUT FASTING AND PRAYING? We are given many examples in the Scriptures of people fasting and praying, especially before meeting a crisis or inaugurating an important work.

When Ezra the prophet saw the unfaithfulness of the chosen people of God, he fasted and prayed as he confessed the sins of the people and his prayer brought about a revival: 'While Ezra was praying and confessing, weeping and throwing himself down before the house of God, a large crowd of Israelites — men, women and children — gathered around him. They too wept bitterly.'[28]

When Nehemiah heard that those who had gone to build the walls of Jerusalem were beset by enemies and misfortune he applied himself to prayer and fasting: 'When I heard these things, I sat down and wept. For some days I mourned and fasted and prayed before the God of heaven.'[29]

IS EVERYONE'S PRAYER ACCEPTED BY GOD? God has given us some very strong counsel about what is and what is not acceptable to Him in fasting and prayer. We read: '''Why have we fasted,' they say, 'and you have not seen it? Why have we humbled ourselves, and you have not noticed?' Yet on the day of your fasting, you do as you please and exploit all your workers. Your fasting ends in quarrelling and strife, and in striking each other with wicked fists. You cannot fast as you do today, and expect your voice to be heard on high.'''[30] ''' . . . Is not this the kind of fasting I have chosen: to loose the chains of injustice and untie the cords of the yoke, to set the oppressed free and break every yoke?'''[31] '''Is it not to share your food with the hungry and to provide the poor wanderer with shelter — when you see the naked, to clothe him, and not to

turn away from your own flesh and blood?'"[32]
"'. . . Then you will call, and the Lord will answer;
you will cry for help, and he will say: Here am I.'"[33]

In certain cases God has told the prophets not to
pray for the people: '"Do not pray for this people nor
offer any plea or petition for them, because I will not
listen when they call to me in the time of their
distress."'[34]

God declared that He would not listen to the
prayers of a people who oppressed the poor and treated
the weak without justice or compassion: '"'When I
called, they did not listen; so when they called, I
would not listen,' says the Lord Almighty."'[35]

WHAT KIND OF PEOPLE OUGHT WE TO BE?

Peter described the horrific events that would unfold
just before the second coming of Christ, then he posed
this rhetorical question: '. . . what kind of people
ought you to be?'[36]

We live in an age when entertainment is a necessary
drug which people seem to need in order to get by.
Whether plugged into a Walkman, driving around to
the sound of the car radio, or glued to the television
for hours at a time, many people are spaced out, tuned
in, or hooked up, but they are not prepared to meet
their God.

How many millions will be found on that day
cheering their favourite sports team, or engrossed in a
soap opera on television? The Scriptures give many
signposts, pointing to the coming of the Lord, but
many are not willing to be shaken out of their comfortable
lethargy. How can God get the attention of these
people to prepare them for the crisis ahead? For, '"'As
it was in the days of Noah, so it will be at the coming
of the Son of Man. For in the days before the flood,

people were eating and drinking, marrying and giving in marriage, up to the day Noah entered the ark; and they knew nothing about what would happen until the flood came and took them all away. That is how it will be at the coming of the Son of Man."'[37]

A lifestyle in which there is heavy dependence on a daily fare of sex, violence, crime and materialism effectively shuts out the voice of God and robs the viewer of the faculties of independent thought and action, while blinding him to his spiritual danger.

We will hear God's voice and be able to discern His will for our lives when our minds are clear to receive divine impressions, and if we wish to maintain a spiritual relationship with our Divine Creator then we must shun any 'entertainment' which does not inspire us in godliness and purity. Jesus said, '"Blessed are the pure in heart, for they will see God."'[38] Only pure hearts have the capacity to meditate on the goodness of our Creator God who made us in His image and for companionship with Him. The Apostle Peter seemed to have said it best: 'The end of all things is near. Therefore be clear minded and self-controlled so that you can pray.'[39]

If you want to know whether you are 'hooked' on watching television, try going a week or a month without switching on once. If time seems to hang heavily and your will-power is sorely challenged, you need to go to your quiet place of prayer and plead to be set free from the habit.

My husband and I tried this test some years ago and discovered that we were very vulnerable to the 'squawk box'. Hence we made a deliberate decision to put it out of our home. There was a noticeable void in our lives at first until we found other, more positive ways to pass the time. We started a programme of walks in areas which enabled our minds to meditate on the God of nature. Our physical health also improved! We found ourselves developing a more positive mental attitude. This improved our self-confidence. The greatest blessing came from improved communication which leads to greater understanding of each other and, consequently, we became more united and harmonious. Our faith in God grew as our thoughts focused more on His goodness demonstrated by His creation and His daily providence. We became conscious of how good life was, reminding us of the words of Jesus: '"I have come that they might have life, and have it to the full."'[40]

As we are the Lord's possession and dwelling place, we owe Him our best service. He has first call on our strength, our intellect and our soul.

Paul declared: 'Do you not know that your body is a temple of the Holy Spirit, who is in you, whom you have received from God? You are not your own; you were bought at a price. Therefore honour God with your body.'[41]

Dear Reader, you too will become more aware of the presence of Jesus in your life and find amazing answers to your every request. For He said, '"Before they call I will answer; while they are still speaking I will hear."'[42]

[1]Acts 10:34. [2]Isaiah 56:7. [3]James 5:16, KJV. [4]2 Chronicles 7:14. [5]Isaiah 1:18. [6]Psalm 139:4, 6. [7]1 Kings 3:11-14, paraphrased. [8]John 14:13. [9]See Matthew 6:32. [10]Romans 3:23; 6:23. [11]John 3:16, KJV. [12]Hebrews 11:6. [13]Psalm 103:14. [14]Jeremiah 29:11, 12. [15]2 Kings 20:5. [16]Jeremiah 31:3. [17]John 16:24. [18]John 14:6. [19]John 14:13, 14. [20]Romans 5:1, 2. [21]Hebrews 4:16. [22]Isaiah 55:11. [23]Daniel 9:20, 21. [24]2 Kings 20:4, 5. [25]Hebrews 10:17. [26]Isaiah 44:22. [27]Galatians 2:20. [28]Ezra 10:1. [29]Nehemiah 1:4. [30]Isaiah 58:3, 4. [31]Verse 6. [32]Verse 7. [33]Verse 9. [34]Jeremiah 11:14; 7:16. [35]Zechariah 7:13. [36]2 Peter 3:11. [37]Matthew 24:37-39. [38]Matthew 5:8. [39]1 Peter 4:7. [40]John 10:10. [41]1 Corinthians 6:19, 20. [42]Isaiah 65:24.